". . . This history offers what no academic treatment of the subject can: passion and the wisdom of experience."

—Roberto Lovato, New America Media

"Told in the voice of the 'voiceless' . . . *Flight to Freedom* brings alive an epic human journey. . . . This book teaches us important lessons about community organizing and empowerment, and the capacity of the human spirit to endure and prevail."

—Michele Prichard, Director of Change Initiatives,
Liberty Hill Foundation, Los Angeles

"This is an important story that must be told. . . . *Flight to Freedom* documents the impressive community-building efforts of the Salvadoran community to gain freedom and have a strong presence in their new adopted land. In Los Angeles they now represent a vibrant segment of the local populace and their contribution to this nation continues to evolve and will surely reinforce the multicultural strength that is the foundation of the United States."

—Ed P. Reyes, Los Angeles City Councilman

Flight to Freedom

The Story of Central American Refugees in California

Edited by

Rossana Pérez with
Henry A. J. Ramos

English translation by Carolina Villarroel

Arte Público Press
Houston, Texas

This volume is made possible through grants from the Charles Stewart Mott Foundation, the City of Houston through the Houston Arts Alliance, the Exemplar Program, a program of Americans for the Arts in collaboration with the LarsonAllen Public Services Group, funded by the Ford Foundation, the James Irvine Foundation, and the Rockefeller Foundation.

Recovering the past, creating the future

University of Houston
Arte Público Press
452 Cullen Performance Hall
Houston, Texas 77204-2004

Cover design by Exact Type
Photos courtesy of Marvin Andrade, Director of CARECEN; Oscar López, Human Resource Coordinator at Clínica Msg. Oscar A. Romero; Rocío Veliz, Technology Coordinator at CARECEN; and Carlos Vaquerano.

Pérez, Rossana
Flight to freedom: the story of Central American refugees in California / by Rossana Pérez; edited, with an introduction, by Henry A. J. Ramos; English translation by Carolina Villarroel.
p. cm.
ISBN: 978-1-55885-329-4 (alk. paper)
1. Refugees—United States—California. 2. Refugees—Central America—Inteviews 3. Refugees—El Salvador—Interviews. 4. Refugees—Services for—United States—California. I. Ramos, Henry, 1959- II. Title.
HV640.4.U54P47 2007
305.868′728407940922—dc22

2007019240
CIP

∞ The paper used in this publication meets the requirements of the American National Standard for Information Sciences—Permanence of Paper for Printed Library Materials, ANSI Z39.48-1984.

7 8 9 0 1 2 3 4 5 6 10 9 8 7 6 5 4 3 2 1

For Sara, Tonatiuh and Sage.
They are the light of the future.

Acknowledgments

I would like to express my gratitude to the people and organizations that helped bring this book to light with their trust, counsel and support. To Henry A. J. Ramos, principal editor, for his patience and guidance through the process; to Roberto Lovato for his insights and recommendations; to Carlos Vaquerano for his support in contacting the participants in the Bay Area; to Marvin Andrade and Rocio Veliz from CARECEN, for their kindness in allowing me to look into their photo archives; to Ricardo Garcia O'Meiney for his art work, to Dr. Nicolás Kanellos and Gabriela Baeza Ventura of Arte Público Press, for their ongoing support; to Anne Mello for conducting my interview; to Sara E. Aguilar, my oldest daughter, for not being afraid to correct my grammar; and to my husband, Michael, for his kindness in helping me at each step of this process.

Finally, I thank Javier Huete, Alicia Mendoza, Carmen Alegría, Carlos Antonio Hernández Vaquerano, Isabel Beltrán Orantes, Eduardo Antonio González Martínez and Juan Ramón Cardona for sharing their stories with me and making the dream of this book a reality.

Table of Contents

Preface

As I reflect on the stories of the eight participants featured in the anthology that follows, I recall when I started to think about writing a book about Salvadorans in California. It was the summer of 2004. I was persuaded that there were many powerful yet untold stories residing among the various Salvadoran community leaders around the state of California. I felt strongly that if these stories could somehow be made public it would greatly increase appreciation of our community's many contributions to American civic culture. To gain support for my idea, I reached out to Roberto Lovato, the former executive director of CARECEN, Los Angeles's leading Central American community advocacy organization. Roberto responded enthusiastically to my idea. He even shared with me his own long-held desire to put together a book about the emerging Salvadoran American population, which he agreed had been grossly under-chronicled in books written about the violence and unrest that rocked El Salvador and brought over a million refugees to California and other states in the 1980s. Roberto, now a contributing editor with New America Media in New York, confirmed my conviction that a book about the Salvadoran American community's recent experiences in the United States would be an important addition to the public record.

By October we had scheduled a meeting to discuss further the prospects of producing a first voice book about Salvadorans in the United States with Henry A. J. Ramos, editor of the Arte Público Press Hispanic Civil Rights Series, and Carlos Vaquerano, another former CARECEN executive who is now running the Salvadoran American Leadership Education Fund (SALEF). They both liked the idea and Henry asked me to send him something in writing at my earliest convenience. He also designated me as the project principal to develop and complete a set of interviews with leading Salvadorans who had been among the first generation of refugees to leave El Salvador in search of a better life in California. By December we had put together a project proposal, for which Henry helped us to gain approval and funding through Arte Público Press under the direction of Dr. Nicolás Kanellos at the University of Houston.

With the project approved, I began 2005 working hard to develop a list of prospective interviewees and a questionnaire, which I shared with different people in the community for input. Using a standard question set was intended to facilitate the flow of the interviews conducted and to logically inform the book's contents. Of course, by definition, the stories are different by virtue of the interviewees' variations in age, geographical origins in El Salvador and diverse dates of arrival in the United States. But the use of a common question set enabled us finally to weave together commonalities in perspective on the Salvadoran experience in California that lift up shared lessons for all of us to consider when reflecting upon the larger context that informed their flight to the United States—their flight to freedom.

During the first months of 2005, I completed agreements with seven other individuals to complete interviews for the anthology. This was an extraordinary process. To begin, I made a conscious decision to select people who were pioneers in forming California's leading Central American community organizations, particularly during the early years, in the 1980s. In selecting interview subjects, moreover, I wanted to highlight individuals who continued to work in the community at some level. Carlos Vaquerano suggested early on that we should talk to several leaders from San Francisco: Carmen Alegría, Alicia Mendoza and Ramón Cardona. Following Carlos' instincts, we flew up together from Los Angeles on a weekend in early March and met with these leading Salvadoran community advocates at a Mexican restaurant in Oakland. After a couple of hours, we all agreed that I would come back soon to formally interview them for the book.

By mid-April, I was back in the Bay Area. I drove to Palo Alto to interview Carmen. The next day, I drove to Concord to interview Alicia. I ended my trip interviewing Ramón in Oakland. The stories and experiences recounted were rich and poignant, both individually and collectively. In each case, drawing on our standard question set, I used a cassette tape recorder to capture verbatim the respondents' comments and insights related to the major topics and themes I wanted to cover. Broadly stated, the essential content I wanted them to speak to included their history in El Salvador, the circumstances that had politicized them and brought them to California, their early and continuing involvements in civic organizations here in the United States, the lessons of their experiences to date and their hopes and dreams for the future.

A similar process informed the book's development in Southern California. I contacted potential contributors and asked if they would consider contributing to the anthology. In virtually every case, the individuals I approached agreed to contribute by telling their stories: Isabel Beltrán, Javier Huete, Eduardo González and, of course, Carlos Vaquerano. My own story is also included here as one of the eight featured entries. Because I was centrally involved in the work highlighted throughout the book, and in order to ensure that my experiences too could help educate and inform the broader public about the Salvadoran community's recent experiences in California, I felt it important to contribute as well.

While securing interviews for the book was surprisingly easy as a logistical matter, it was emotionally difficult. At every step along the way, I was reminded that numerous leaders who had played instrumental roles in our formation as a community in California some twenty-five years ago had since either returned to El Salvador, migrated to other places or passed away. Reflecting back on their passages with those of us who remain in California was humbling and bittersweet. Many of these people had been instrumental in and even essential to our struggle. It was hard for me not to become particularly emotional thinking about the larger losses that had marked the generation of which we had all emerged in El Salvador. During the 1980s and early 1990s, the U.S.-backed war in our country left more than 80,000 people dead and more than 9,000 individuals "disappeared."

Given all that our community has experienced as a result of being ripped in and from our homeland more than a generation ago, the completion of this anthology is a dream come true. This is especially the case for those of us who have lived on the front edge of resistance and reformation relative to El Salvador's national policies and American engagement in the region. I remember that during the solidarity and sanctuary years of the 1980s we always talked about documenting history in the making, but at that time we had too much work in front of us to do so. For virtually all of us, there were endless meetings and actions intended to stop the war in our country. There were many sleepless nights, many obstacles to overcome. At the same time, we were all desperately trying to find a legal safe haven in the United States—something that U.S. policy of the day made almost impossible.

Notwithstanding the many hardships we have faced as a community in recent decades, we have found a way to thrive and evolve. Although the California Salvadoran community is a fairly new participant in U.S. civic life, its contributions to California and the nation's political, social and economic advancement have been enormous. There are now over 1 million Salvadorans residing in California and the Salvadoran community's leadership includes important political figures like former California state senator Liz Figueroa, as well as noted journalists such as Ruben Martínez and entertainers like Efran Ramírez. In addition, California, now home to some 60 percent of the U.S. Salvadoran population, produces billions of dollars in national consumer and tax revenue from Salvadorans and over $1 billion in annual direct aid to El Salvador through private family remittances.

This book is an attempt to compile and share the first person stories of leaders who helped to form the anchor organizations that provided, and through the years continued to provide, support to the California Salvadoran community. The variety of insights they have to share reflects the diversity of the community at large. Their common thread is the desire for a better society and the shared sense of need to work, accordingly, for social justice.

The stories featured here principally relate to individual experiences in a country in turmoil. The contributors share how each of us and our families were affected by civil war in El Salvador—a conflict that lasted for more than a decade. As we tell our stories, memories of a deeply divided country and fragmented families surface: fragmented both by competing ideologies and by the distances that increasingly separated us as many fled to the United States in search of a better life while others stayed behind. All of these past realities clearly remain fresh in our memories as lasting legacies of the war.

Flight to Freedom serves as a collective testament—a testament to the power of people to seek and make change. After the Peace Agreements took place in El Salvador in the early 1990s, leading Salvadoran community organizations in the United States had to redirect their work efforts in order to better respond to the new realities of community members who had chosen to make their lives here in this country. For a variety of reasons, most of the Salvadorans who came to the United States to flee war and political persecution decided to remain here when the Salvadoran conflict ended. Many are considered still to be illegal U.S. residents despite having laid strong roots and allegiances in America. The issue of immigration is thus still unresolved. Over the years, there have been different amnesty programs offered, yet all of these have somehow contained major loopholes that have locked Salvadorans and others out of the possibility of obtaining permanent residency.

Despite the continuing hurdles, Salvadorans in California and elsewhere have continued to build and to fight for their survival. The Caja de Crédito (a people's credit union and economic development corporation) was formed in 1997, based on the community's need for supportive economic development. The need to educate people about civic participation through the work of groups like SALEF, and to encourage higher education for the next generations, have become priorities in order to ensure our increased representation and progress in key aspects of U.S. life. In this connection, the nation's first Central American Studies Program was created in 1999 at California State University at Northridge (CSUN). Like this book, the Program serves the need to educate younger Salvadoran Americans—and others—about our history, as well as to prepare them for important future leadership roles in our community and in the larger culture, through the benefit of a more informed understanding of who we are.

As we enter the twenty first century, our communities both in El Salvador and in the United States still have a lot of unfinished business to face from the war period. Until now, those responsible for many of the massacres and political crimes that took place have not been brought to justice. But neither the Salvadoran community nor the larger American family can live much longer in denial of this history. Our history needs to be acknowledged and a healing process through dialogue should take place. Silence will not change the legacy of destruction and horror that we witnessed; revisiting that history openly and honestly is the only way that we can assure it will not happen again.

Fifteen years after the Peace Agreements there is still not a solution in sight to address increasing poverty in El Salvador. Official terror perpetrated by the state has mutated into organized crime and gang violence throughout the country. The more than $1 billion in annual remittances sent by U.S.-based Salvadorans are increasingly depended on to support the core economy of the country. Due to the resulting lack of job opportunities, the remaining Salvadorans back home are increasingly immigrating to the United States with the hope of finding economic opportunity. But in the current anti-immigrant environment that characterizes contemporary U.S. public discourse, the American Dream is becoming more and more difficult for these newcomers to achieve since they lack the proper documentation to work.

We are a transnational community; whatever happens in El Salvador affects us here in the United States and vice versa. The stories that make up this book highlight this reality. Through them we connect to history, to the collective memory of our community, the memory of our past, the memory of our pain, the memory that keeps us going. We must share this memory with our children because they are the future and it is our responsibility to provide them with the tools of knowledge that give us a better understanding of our identity.

I hope that readers of all kinds will enjoy and learn from *Flight to Freedom*. Its contents may invoke tears and smiles all at once but, considering what is covered, that is appropriately fitting. These are stories of wisdom and courage in the face of unimaginable challenges. These are the testimonies of those who, facing the turmoil of El Salvador at the close of the twentieth century, had the vision and disposition to take flight to freedom in California. It is a long way from the battlefields of our country to the golden state that stands as the gateway to the American Dream. And yet, as you will see in the pages that follow, the recent experiences of Salvadoran Americans have greatly reduced the distance between these seemingly disconnected places. In effect, the Salvadoran American community has irrevocably bound together these otherwise distant and disconnected points on the map; and we have done so in a manner that is fundamentally constructive and inspiring. Surely there is much for all of us to learn from this culmination of experiences and events.

Rossana Pérez
Los Angeles, CA
June 2007

Introduction

During the 1980s, more than a million men and women from the small Central American nation of El Salvador made their way to the United States. They had been forced to flee their country as a result of a nearly decade-long reign of violence that was visited upon the Salvadoran people by a U.S.-backed, right-wing government. That government, in turn, was supported by a brutal military and an allied network of paramilitary forces that organized systematic assassinations, disappearances and torture to quell dissent of any kind. Students and intellectuals, labor leaders, rural peasants who resisted government domination and, ultimately, those who took up arms to defend themselves were the principal targets of the Salvadoran government's repression.

As the brutality against these groups evolved in El Salvador, government-sponsored violence there extended out in increasingly shocking ways to victims who were hardly classic targets of official action. In a dark series of state-supported atrocities that included highly public mass killings, the violence and terror in El Salvador ultimately led to the brutal rapes and murders of several American Catholic nuns, the assassination of the nation's most popular Catholic Church leader and the slaughter of various Jesuit priests who ran the UCA, a Catholic university that had served thousands of Salvadorans for nearly two decades.

These developments, coupled with the death or disappearance of nearly 100,000 Salvadorans dating back to the 1970s, outraged American religious leaders and liberals. That outrage in turn inspired strong mobilizations against the Salvadoran ruling regime through a Solidarity Movement intended to support resistance efforts in El Salvador and to put pressure on American leaders to cease all but humanitarian foreign aid to that country. It also resulted in a well organized Sanctuary Movement that built on a series of localized and largely church-led efforts to provide safe haven to Salvadorans in the United States who, though at risk of official retaliation in El Salvador for their anti-government political views, were nevertheless being targeted by American immigration officials for repatriation to their nation of origin.

At the time, the conservative Reagan administration asserted that the Salvadoran government's tactics were merely responsive to communist infiltration and subversion efforts that were being financed by Cuba and the Soviet Union throughout Central America. On this assertion, the American government provided substantial financial support, equipment and training to the Salvadoran government and military, as well as other pro-U.S. states and armies throughout the region. This support was ostensibly intended to repress the purported communist insurgencies gaining traction there with outside interference and instigation.

In fact, the conflicts that beset Central America during this period —in nations including not only El Salvador, but also Guatemala and Nicaragua—would more accurately have been labeled internal civil wars. These conflicts were the product of more than one hundred years of North American and European imperialism, and a plethora of institutionalized inequalities and injustices that had resulted for the majority of people throughout the region. In El Salvador, the efforts of the people to question and ultimately challenge these realities, dating back to the 1930s, were crushed to the degree that anyone remaining in active opposition to the ruling establishment by the mid-1970s was subject to state-supported terror.

Rational people from all backgrounds and regions of El Salvador who had any way to get out of the country during these years made every effort to do so. The early 1980s thus saw a discernible spike in the numbers of Salvadoran people pursuing security and new opportunities outside of their country. With relatively few exceptions, those who left El Salvador during this exodus did so clandestinely, on the run. They became political refugees trapped between the brutally repressive agencies of their national government and the mainly unwelcoming police and border security forces of surrounding nations.

As a result of this massive flight to freedom, Salvadorans were suddenly dispersed throughout the Western hemisphere. Some ended up succeeding in gaining access to neighboring countries, including

Honduras, Mexico and Canada, where they made new lives for themselves. The majority of those who left El Salvador, however, made their way to a handful of U.S. cities, including among them Houston, New Orleans, Washington, DC, Miami, Boston and New York. But the American cities that by far received the largest numbers of Salvadoran transplants were California's most populated centers: Los Angeles and San Francisco.

Over half of all the people who fled El Salvador during the 1980s came to California to seek freedom from the violence that had besieged their nation. In some measure this was a byproduct of several prior waves of Salvadoran immigrants who had successfully made their way to California in search of employment after the conclusion of World War II. In other respects, the Salvadoran refugees' preference for the West Coast had to do with the magnetic draw of California for people all over the world that stemmed from its historical status as a leading generator of cultural innovation and opportunity.

While the Salvadorans who came to California and other parts of the United States in the 1980s had left El Salvador to avoid death and persecution—legitimate bases for them to have been protected under international law as political refugees, the Reagan administration and its successor, the first Bush administration, refused to recognize them as such. Virtually none of the Salvadoran citizens who sought legal asylum protection in the United States during this period were thus granted such status. For the U.S. government to have seriously entertained and accommodated the many thousands of Salvadoran asylum applications submitted during these years would have been a contradiction in terms, an admission that the U.S.-backed Salvadoran government was in fact an abusive, anti-democratic outlaw regime, rather than the peace loving, pro-democracy stalwart that conservative Americans had painted it to be.

The massive resettlement of Salvadorans in California and other places across the United States during the 1980s required heroic community-based mutual support efforts to meet the newcomers' basic survival requirements and legal advocacy needs. The essential impulse of this organizing campaign was two-fold in nature: to protect the arriving refugees from the real potential of physical endangerment as a result of repatriation to El Salvador, on one hand, and to enable these individuals to remain and work in this country pending a resolution of the crisis in El Salvador, on the other hand. Salvadoran men and women of various backgrounds emerged to lead these efforts, which were both daunting and inspiring at once.

Most of these newfound leaders had been firsthand victims of state repression back home and most of them were relatively young. On average, the individuals who emerged to establish the U.S. Salvadoran refugee community's early leadership during this period were only in their twenties and thirties. Many of these leaders had experienced unspeakable violations and loss in El Salvador; almost all of them, moreover, had undertaken Herculean, indeed life-threatening risks in order to make their way to the United States. Despite the enormous continuing personal costs of their respective journeys, their relative lack of English language skills and their limited knowledge about the American political system, they found a way over the ensuing years to make crucial contributions to American foreign and human rights policy, a well as U.S. civic culture.

In pursuing this work, the young Salvadoran refugees inspired collaboration and support for their cause in many important circles of power in this nation. By the mid-1980s, they had enlisted the active support of leading U.S. entertainment figures, as well as progressive political leaders, intellectuals and conscientious professionals in fields ranging from law to medicine. In partnership with these and other allies, the young Salvadoran leaders and constituencies behind the Solidarity and Sanctuary Movements ultimately prevailed in influencing a cessation of the violence and repression in El Salvador by the early 1990s. Along the way, they also successfully secured a legal temporary protected status for Salvadoran émigrés to the United States that ultimately shaped U.S. law in more flexible directions of benefit to other refugee populations throughout Latin America.

In addition to these impressive achievements, the leaders of the Salvadoran refugee community in the United States built from scratch during this period and evolved in subsequent years important, high performing community service and organizing institutions that, over time, have contributed mightily to the vitality of U.S. community and public life. Among these institutions have been groups like CARECEN (the Central American Resource Center), El Rescate (The Rescue), Clínica Msr. Oscar A. Romero and SALEF (the Salvadoran American Leadership and Educational Fund). Building on these institutional bases, Salvadoran community principals developed during the early-to-mid-1990s model community service and outreach programs in partnership with important mainstream institutions, including private foundations and corporations like the James Irvine Foundation, ARCO and the Liberty Hill Foundation. They also galvanized increased attention to the Salvadoran refugee community's presence and concerns at important regional institutions of higher learning such as UCLA and California State University, Northridge, the latter of which recently established the nation's first degree granting program in Central American studies.

Among the leaders who helped to make this work and its resulting achievements possible was Irma Rossana Pérez. As an early principal of Los Angeles's Comité Santana Chirino Amaya (a group that eventually informed the development of what was to become El Rescate and Clínica Msr. Oscar A. Romero), Pérez was then known by the alias Sara Martínez. Many of the Salvadoran leaders of the era used aliases to protect themselves and their families from the still-long reach of the Salvadoran government and it's supporting paramilitary forces. Pérez was a middle-class woman who had grown up in the suburbs of San Salvador, El Salvador's capitol city. She had been forced to flee El Salvador when the worst of the madness affecting that nation touched her own life in the early 1980s.

Pérez's engagement with a revolutionary university student organization in El Salvador that included her then-husband and fellow student resistance leader had resulted in the two of them being targeted as subversives. One day, her young husband was kidnapped and disappeared, never to be seen again. Shortly thereafter, Pérez herself was abducted by Salvadoran security forces, tortured and then, imprisoned. Through the good fortune of a negotiated amnesty for certain political prisoners orchestrated by moderate Christian Democratic minority leaders in the Salvadoran government, Pérez was able to gain an early prison release. Soon afterwards, she was able to flee to Mexico and then to the United States, with her young daughter and a sister.

Upon her eventual resettlement in Los Angeles, Pérez worked quickly to reconnect with Salvadoran community members and resistance leaders. Within weeks of her arrival she became involved in a variety of emerging mutual support organizations and networks that she ultimately helped to strengthen and build with other Salvadoran refugees involved in the struggle. In the process, she sacrificed considerably in terms of the sheer amount of work in which she engaged, the risks she assumed in relation to potential further Salvadoran government retaliation (even in the United States), and the considerable time she lost in connection with pursuing a normal family and private life.

I met Rossana Pérez, as she is now known, under the alias "Sara Martínez" in 1992. I was a young program officer at the James Irvine Foundation. I had just assumed major new responsibilities for the foundation's emerging program in civic culture, which was essentially designed to establish various new multi-million dollar initiatives on California race relations, immigration and civic participation issues. My first meeting with Pérez occurred in the aftermath of the 1992 riots that erupted in Los Angeles following the initial verdict in Rodney King's celebrated police beating case. She was actively involved in community recovery efforts affecting the Pico-Union District of Los Angeles, which along with Koreatown and South Central Los Angeles had been disproportionately impacted by the civil unrest resulting from the King verdict.

Pérez was one of the key people involved in the Salvadoran community and its anchor nonprofit institutions during this period, and she graciously played a large role in helping to introduce me to the Salvadoran people's recent history and evolution in southern California. Carlos Vaquerano and, later, Roberto Lovato, of CARECEN, both close colleagues of Pérez, as well as Oscar Andrade of El Rescate, also became key informants who helped to educate me about the U.S. Salvadoran community's many pressing issues.

These leaders did me a great service to take the time to bring me along—as they did other important civic leaders struggling to catch up with Los Angeles's rapidly shifting social, economic, cultural and political landscapes in the early 1990s. Despite my Mexican American background and long time interest in U.S. immigration policy issues, I knew embarrassingly little about Salvadorans back then. Like most southern Californians who had not been heavily involved in the Solidarity and Sanctuary Movements, I was surprised to learn in the weeks and months following the 1992 riots that Pico-Union housed the largest Salvadoran population in the world outside of San Salvador. I was also surprised to learn how sophisticated and yet grossly under-resourced the leading Salvadoran community organizations were in relation to the highly demanding and complicated work they had been called on to undertake since their still only recent inceptions.

With help and information that I received from Rossana Pérez and other Salvadoran community leaders during this period, I was able to successfully advance the first major private foundation grants ever directed to CARECEN and El Rescate. The James Irvine Foundation's support for these groups involved grants totaling in each case $150,000, to assist the respective organizations in consolidating their core infrastructure and expanding their public influence through increased communications and domestic policy advocacy. This funding probably would not have been possible to secure without the coaching that Pérez and her fellow community leaders provided to me.

Happily, the Irvine Foundation grants that I helped to shepherd through for these organizations had an important catalytic affect within the larger private philanthropy field. In due course, over the next two years, CARECEN and El Rescate were able to receive comparable first time grants from other important regional foundations ranging from the Riordan Foundation to the Ralph E. Parsons Foundation. In time, CARECEN was additionally successful in securing for the first time ever important national funding from my former employer, the Ford Foundation. These combined developments played an essential role in helping to leverage the U.S. Salvadoran community's transition from a temporary, refugee status population to a more permanent new American community that was fast-growing and increasingly seen as relevant to key U.S. leaders and power brokers.

In the years that followed my personal involvement in observing and supporting the California Salvadoran community's early development, I returned to other interests and work—first in the San Francisco Bay Area and then in New York City. In both places, I had considerable prior life experiences and relationships that drew me back. Because of these moves, I maintained only sporadic contact with my Salvadoran American friends in Los Angeles and I lost touch with Rossana Pérez altogether. But, even in far away San Francisco and

New York, I would often find myself thinking of my past work with these leading Los Angeles figures and wondering what had become of them, including especially Pérez.

It was therefore extremely welcome and ironic, one day in 2005, to receive an unexpected call from Roberto Lovato, the ex-executive director of CARECEN, requesting the opportunity to put me back in touch with Rossana Pérez. Lovato indicated that Pérez wanted to share with me a book concept she had been thinking about. Nearly a decade had passed since our last communication with one another; yet it was like our last conversation had been only yesterday. It was easy for me to agree to Lovato's proposed conversation with Pérez.

When I called Pérez back a day or two later, she and I also quickly reconnected. She told me that she had learned through our mutual friends Roberto Lovato and Carlos Vaquerano (another former CARECEN executive who was now heading up SALEF), that I was living in New York and editing a series of books on Latino civil and human rights history. She then told me a bit about the book that she had in mind to write. She explained to me that her motivation was to do something about the still insufficiently documented experiences and civic contributions of the Salvadoran American refugee leaders that she had worked with back in the 1980s and 1990s. She wanted me to help get her book published.

Her timing could not have been better. I was in fact just completing a seminal book series on modern Hispanic civil rights history in the United States as an executive editor in collaboration with the University of Houston's Arte Público Press. Ironically, I had recently been searching for a way to include a volume on Salvadoran Americans' important experiences and contributions relative to this history. Our series had produced to that point nearly twenty-five new books, mainly on notable but under-chronicled Mexican-American leaders, organizations and movements that had informed critically important advancements in twentieth century U.S. social justice. We had also produced under the series various important new books on Puerto Rican and Cuban American social justice history in the United States. But, to date, we had not produced anything on the very important and dramatic social justice history of post-WW II Salvadorans and other

Central Americans in the United States Rossana Pérez's proposal gave us the opportunity to correct this glaring oversight.

Pérez and I agreed to meet a few weeks later when I was planning to be out in Los Angeles again on business. We also agreed to include Lovato and Vaquerano in our discussions, in order to ensure a full consideration of how Pérez's proposed work could best achieve community benefit, as well as the scholarly significance that Arte Público Press sought to encourage through its Hispanic Civil Rights Series. Pérez, Lovato and Vaquerano later met with me, accordingly, at the Bonaventure Hotel in downtown Los Angeles. Our first meeting ended favorably but with a lack of a clear consensus on how the envisioned book might best be completed.

One contingent of discussion participants thought the book should be a popular collection of interviews or narratives featuring the first-voice testimonies of selected Salvadoran immigrants regarding their achievements and impacts during the late 1980s and early 1990s. Another contingent thought it should be a more scholarly and critical work, examining the lessons of the Salvadoran refugee community's experience (including failures and shortcomings) for current and future community education purposes. In addition, our preliminary discussions produced a lack of consensus as to whether the project should be led by a single designated lead project director or, rather, a small committee of co-directors.

In the end, following a series of additional phone and email exchanges, I decided to suggest that the book be organized by a single designated project director as a collection of interviews, based on a common question set targeted to selected Salvadoran refugee leaders who had helped to establish the community in Los Angeles. Because the original instinct to produce a book on the Salvadoran community of southern California had been Pérez's, I also suggested that she serve as the project's point person. After some brief discussion, we reached a general buy in on the aforementioned concepts, with important caveats expressed, however, by both Lovato and Vaquerano.

Roberto Lovato urged a degree of attention to intellectual rigor and consistency in the subject matter to be covered in the book—a common list of questions, a constructively critical eye in reporting and the like; he wanted to ensure the product's meaningful contribution to the scholarly record. For his part, Carlos Vaquerano insisted that the book's coverage should extend as well to northern California leaders who had been essential to the Salvadoran community's recent political evolution in the United States. At the end of this exchange to define the proposed book's appropriate organization and content, we ended up with an agreement.

Specifically, we agreed to build the book around a set of six to eight targeted interviewees from both southern and northern California, and a common set of key questions to be universally administered by Pérez throughout the entire interview process. We also agreed that both Pérez and Vaquerano should be included among the interviewees for the volume, given their central participation in the California Salvadoran community's institution building and advocacy work over the years.

In order to gain the buy-in necessary to pursue the project along these lines with meaningful statewide participation and support, Pérez and Vaquerano agreed to schedule a meeting with three or four additional Salvadoran leaders who were key early refugee community advocates in the San Francisco Bay Area. Several months following our initial conversations in Los Angeles, Pérez and Vaquerano thus traveled to San Francisco to meet with the various Bay Area Salvadoran leaders featured herein, to inform them about the project and to encourage their involvement. Their ideas and invitation were received with enthusiasm.

Further consultations between the project's primary subjects produced a protocol of agreed questions around which to organize formal interviews so as to provide focus and continuity in relation to the book's ultimate content. These consultations led to a particular pattern and practice in the interview completion process. The questions developed were decidedly intended to encourage each interview subject to go back to his or her early experiences in El Salvador, to trace the circumstances that led to each individual's eventual exodus to California and to assess their early experiences and continuing expectations in the United States.

The questions were additionally designed to enable interviewees to clarify the ways in which they have remained involved (if at all) in community-building activities on behalf of Salvadoran Americans. These questions further probed interview subjects for feedback on the activities in which they became most engaged as U.S.-based Salvadoran advocates. The questions additionally sought to surface each interviewee's sense of the various impacts their activities and engagements had ultimately produced looking back on things with the benefit of time and perspective. A final set of questions solicited interviewees' thoughts about the future that awaits them still, as well as that of the larger Salvadoran American community.

Project participants also came together during this time to agree that each interview to be conducted for the book would be tape recorded and then transcribed for editing and final publication. As a practical matter, because the interviewees were overwhelmingly primary Spanish speakers, it was agreed early on that virtually all of the interviews would be conducted—and so recorded—in Spanish and, then, translated into English for subsequent editing and interviewee review and approval prior to going into final publication. In fact, this basic protocol was consistently and successfully followed throughout the project's implementation.

When participating Salvadoran American leaders had finally reached these basic agreements about the book project's proposed content and methodological approach, I put Rossana Pérez directly in touch with Arte Público Press publisher Dr. Nicolás Kanellos at the University of Houston. Within a couple of weeks, he had a joint phone conversation with Pérez and Vaquerano and the decision was made to conclude a book contract, with Pérez designated to serve as the legal author. In subsequent consultations with Vaquerano and Lovato, Pérez finalized a list of eight project interviewees, as well as a common set of questions for each of them to answer in tape recorded interviews of approximately one hour in duration.

Over the course of several months thereafter Pérez conducted all but her own formal taped interview. In the case of Pérez's testimonial, a former colleague named Anne Mello played the role of interviewer. When each of the original interview transcripts was presented in translated English format, I comprehensively edited the text for readability and flow, leaving the essential substance and "voice" of each entry to the best of my ability while also striving toward some degree of continuity in basic style throughout. To the extent that anything has been lost or any fact unwittingly misrepresented through this process, the blame and responsibility are entirely mine.

While I am inherently biased, given my proximity to the leaders and the spirit that brought this publication forward, I firmly believe it is impossible to read this work without gaining a much clearer appreciation of the featured leaders' courage, moral integrity and wisdom. These are extraordinary people who have experienced and achieved extraordinary things in their lifetimes. They have faced conditions and circumstances in the course of their journey, both in El Salvador as well as in this country, that lesser people could never have survived. They have accomplished major successes in relation to forging the productive new lives and the impressive institutions they have created in this nation. And they have done these many important things virtually against all odds. Considering where they came from and what they came to, their hard work, vision and grace are nothing less than awe-inspiring.

In these times of growing anti-immigrant sentiment in the United States and other industrialized nations of the world, it is especially important to reflect on the lessons provided by the experiences of individuals like the Salvadoran refugee leaders featured in this volume. These lessons reveal the many societal benefits of immigrants and refugees gaining access to more privileged nations like ours and modeling in ways that many of the rest of us have lost touch with what it means to be free—free to express our political viewpoints; free to build new and ever-better lives, institutions and possibilities; free to live with purpose in the relative absence of terror and injustice. For too many of us who are not recent refugees or immigrants, these aspects of our freedom have simply become too easy to take for granted.

Against this backdrop, books like this one play a critical informing role in raising public consciousness and encouraging still-needed social justice reforms in our nation and throughout the world. Younger readers—both Hispanic and non-Hispanic—who did not directly experience the particularly harsh realities that gave rise to the Salvadoran Diaspora of the 1980s should especially benefit from exposure to this story. By reading *Flight to Freedom: The Story of Central American Refugees in California* young readers especially may be able to take into greater consideration than otherwise possible, the profound value and benefits of living in a still relatively free and open society. They may contemplate pursuing an activist path in law, education or community and labor organizing in order to play a role in preserving the distinguishing aspects of our democratic culture, including especially protecting the rights of society and the world's most vulnerable people.

Younger people reading the stories herein may furthermore gain insight into how much commitment, patience and hard work is often required to forge even the most basic advancements in civil and human rights. They may be made to realize in ways they had not thought of before that change—especially needed and important societal change—is extremely hard to come by. And, yet, at the same time, reading the testimonies of the interviewees featured here throughout may simultaneously alert younger readers of this volume that change is nevertheless achievable. In this way, they may gain a deeper appreciation of their own unrealized power and opportunity in contemporary society, and a stronger sense of potential and responsibility to assume a degree of leadership in shaping the social justice history still to be made.

The Arte Público Press Hispanic Civil Rights Series that makes this publication possible seeks to educate, inform and inspire Americans of all backgrounds, especially younger Americans—by lifting up the U.S. Latino community's many important contributions to, and struggles for justice in, America. With support in recent years from private grant makers including the James Irvine Foundation, the Charles Stewart Mott Foundation, the Rockefeller Foundation, the Ewing Marion Kauffman Foundation, The California Wellness Foundation, The California Endowment, Carnegie Corporation of New York and Prudential Financial, the Series is producing more than twenty original works by and about many of the leading protagonists of Latino America's post-World War II civil rights history.

Raising awareness about these informing, but still remarkably under-chronicled chapters in U.S. social advancement is more important than ever, as Latinos have emerged to become the nation's new minority of record. With now nearly 40 million individuals comprising the national Hispanic community, and a burgeoning youth population that demographers predict will result in fully one in four Americans being of Latino heritage by the year 2050, it is imperative for all citizens and longtime residents of the United States to gain a more evolved comprehension of Hispanic people—and for Hispanic Americans themselves (along with their closest friends and allies) to tell the stories of their experiences and social justice contributions over recent decades.

By bringing forward these affirmative stories and the voices of leaders who have helped to shape them, Arte Público Press seeks to develop the texture of recorded U.S. history in ways that elevate public recognition of the Hispanic role in defining what it means to be an American. It also hopes to encourage expanded public dialogue about the important continuing social justice work that needs still to be advanced in Latino and other communities of the United States that confront enduring inequities.

Flight to Freedom: The Story of Central American Refugees in California is a truly important addition to our series. The book was largely made possible by a generous grant from the San Francisco-based James Irvine Foundation, which, as referenced above, has played a large role over the years in helping to encourage expanded immigrant and refugee integration, as well as civic participation and well being in California. We are most indebted to the Foundation's president James E. Canales, himself the product of a Central American immigrant family, for continuing this tradition through generous support for this publication and others that we are currently completing on California Latino and Latina rights leaders.

Henry A. J. Ramos
Executive Editor, Hispanic Civil Rights Series
July 2007
New York, NY

Carmen Alegría

My memories of the past in El Salvador are often difficult to face. At the same time, these early experiences shaped in me a deep sense of public responsibility that has followed me since. I remember, for example, situations involving family, neighbors and friends that remind me still now, sadly, about what was beginning to happen in El Salvador that ultimately led to war and chaos. For me, an important part of my perspective was shaped by the fact that I was born and largely raised in the United States; but I was significantly exposed to life in El Salvador by virtue of regularly visiting and living there for weeks and months at a time as a child. My frequent contact with circumstances in Central America gave me a unique perspective on social justice issues even back then.

A large part of my family history in El Salvador is informed by a long lineage of successful medical professionals. My cousin, a doctor, followed in this tradition. I would often spend days at his office, learning about his work and helping him here and there. As visitors prepared to come into his medical office, he would take the children first. One day, a lady carrying what I thought was a baby came in. She sat down. My cousin knew her. He asked her if she had been breastfeeding the baby, and she replied no. I stood there staring at the child. Although he was three years old, I confused him with a baby because of his small size, how he hardly moved, his lost eyes and his stiff hair. As I was staring at the baby, I heard some of what my cousin said, but the only thing I could really think about was that the child was obviously dying. My cousin touched him. He talked some more with the woman, the mother. He scolded her. When they left, he said to me, "That little boy is going to die in three or four hours."

There were other malnourished babies who came to my cousin's clinic. In fact, many people who came in were malnourished. There was a community nearby, below a cliff next to the garbage dump on the way to Ilupango, on the way to the old airport. The people my cousin served came from there and I saw all their afflictions: skin diseases, worms that form circles, sickly mothers with their equally ill children. It was truly awful for me, particularly thinking about that first dying child I saw with his mother, because I was right by him. I will never forget that experience.

Something else that I remember, that is quite different but that has made me think a lot was that my family had an estate at the San Salvador volcano, on the other side. On the grounds there was a house and a beautiful garden. There was coffee and a lot of people, settlers all around us who lived there, nearby. We were relatively privileged. By contrast, for the most part, our neighbors were poor. There was a gate that led to our house and inside was a grassy area. During the siesta, as our parents rested, all the kids were left to play ball on our yard. Poor kids from the surrounding area would come to our gate; they would hang on the bars and would ask us to let them in. My cousins would not even look at them. I felt a responsibility in me, however, that I had to do something, that I had to let them in. And so I did.

At the time, I was nine years old. When the neighboring poor children began to come into our yard, my cousins became upset with me and they scolded me. They could not get the visitors out, though, because we had started playing. That memory has stayed with me too, the children's look and mine: I saw them look at our luxurious house. I knew where they were coming from and I also knew their plight as a result of time spent at my cousin's clinic. It was one of those moments when one reflects: "I don't deserve all this. Why do I have it?" In those moments, I did not know why I had so much privilege and I did not like the fact that I did. That sort of feeling impacts your life.

Other things happened. One of our maids had mental problems. Though she never hurt anyone, she would always make strange jokes and create minor embarrassments. One day, her father took her home and tied her to a tree and left her there. The family left her there for years, feeding her occasionally. How was such a thing possible? That impacted me a lot.

Something else that impacted me was the Rosales Psychiatric Hospital, where my grandfather was a doctor and my mother was a nurse. My mother promised me that one day she or my cousin would take me to the psychiatric ward. I believe that she wanted me to understand something about how fortunate we were in comparison to those who had ended up there. My cousin ended up taking me. This was during the 1950s, when I was still a young girl. We went into the ward. There was a small gate and an observation bridge on the second floor where we settled in. All of the patients were on the first floor. Some were naked, some screaming, others laughing uncontrollably. The patients' conditions were terrible.

All of the experiences I recount here from my youth deeply affected me: the little boy who was dying from malnutrition, the poor young people seeking what they did not have at the gate of our family estate, the people in the psychiatric ward who, because they did not have anything when they were born, became frustrated with life. By my early adulthood, I was embarrassed with myself all the time; it was a permanent sensation for being me. I hated my privilege and felt the impulse to do something to somehow change my situation and that of the Salvadoran people.

During that period in El Salvador, we began to learn about the guerrillas fighting for social change in Guatemala. For a moment, I actually wanted to join up with them in the mountains. But that did not happen, of course. Instead, I went back to school in the United States. In the ensuing years, beyond my formal education, I found myself increasingly engaged in religious pursuits. I got involved with Catholic Charities at the encouragement of one of my uncles who was a priest. I also started teaching Sunday school. During these years my politics began to turn increasingly to the left and away from the more conservative orientation I had been raised to follow. My focus, moreover, had turned to the large issues shaping the American political landscape at the time. Even with infrequent visits and contacts in El Salvador, the situation there became more distant to me.

But time and circumstances eventually brought me back to the realities beginning to take hold in El Salvador. During the late 1970s, when the early resistance movements began to appear, the country and even families became divided, including my own. One of my cousins was kidnapped and murdered; he was a foreign minister. I thought: "I don't want to be in the struggle in a country where I will probably have to kill a relative. I don't want to do that. I don't want to see them suffer. They may deserve it, but I don't want to be a part of that." In 1972, I decided that I would not return to El Salvador until I could clarify my political position and that of my family. In the meantime, there were the struggles for change in Guatemala and Nicaragua, and El Salvador was deeply affected by events in both of these neighboring countries. I ultimately decided that I needed to be part of the change that was taking hold throughout the region. That is when I went to Guatemala to work in human rights. I found other Salvadorans there doing the same thing. But before long I was back in El Salvador.

Once re-engaged in the country, I saw that the struggle was just. The combined forces of government and corporate corruption were denying the people's basic rights. My position at the time as a journalist helped to make this clear to me. I worked at a TV station where one evening about eight people arrived to report that they had been beaten up while working as Coca Cola employees. They were bleeding and they came to tell us what happened. It turned out these people had tried to encourage good faith, needed changes in working conditions at their factory, only to be met with official, company-sanctioned violence. From that moment on, I stopped drinking Coca Cola because I saw firsthand the abuse.

There were others like the employees who were abused by Coca Cola. They were working in the fields, picking cotton with planes flying over them fumigating. Many died of cancer at an early age as a result of the pesticides they were forced to ingest. There were other inhumane work conditions that I saw in a machete manufacturing plant where employees had very soft skin because of the hot-fired areas in which they were forced to work. In fact, there were about five furnaces inside the central market in El Salvador alone, all filled with black smoke that polluted the air with toxins that the people working and shopping there had to breathe in. Private interests produced these harms with essentially no concern for the people affected; but, through inaction, government officials created the conditions that enabled these private interests to operate in this way.

These were the circumstances that motivated me and others to do something for the community. Those were the circumstances that inspired us to become activists. I had—we all had—inspiration from others as well who were committed to the cause of justice. Miguel Mármol was a large influence. A woman named Ana María was a more personal role model to me and others who worked with us. She was a particularly effective activist who, like me, became an educator. I was particularly inspired by friends and colleagues who knew the Andes 21 de Junio popular literacy teachings of Pablo Freire, and who were motivated by them.

All of these influences eventually drew me into the Solidarity Movement. I think that notions of solidarity gain life at the same time in small towns and organizations when people all over are challenged to seek better lives and self-defense as a result of increasingly repressive official injustice. Depending on what is happening in one's country, one responds to the needs in solidarity. I started with the disappeared. I participated on several searches for individuals who had been kidnapped or who remained unaccounted for. We went to convents and other safe venues to collect information from family members and friends left behind. I had to interview people who told me of their troubled lives, of who they were and what they had lost as a result of official terror.

There was a woman working with me who was also a journalist. I interviewed her because she worked with the female prisoners. She told us that some nuns knew where abductors were holding people kidnapped and that she wanted to go there. Her name was Irma Flaquer and she was being persecuted because of what she knew. She was a woman who was very outspoken. Her father was a politician. Soon after we met, Irma and I started looking for disappeared people; we found a woman and two young children first. Happily, they were alive.

I soon returned to the United States because, after speaking with many Central American progressives over there, it became obvious that they felt I could be more helpful to their cause living in the United States and securing support from North Americans. Guatemalans and Salvadorans would tell me, "Leave! Go back over there. You can help us from over there." They knew that being born in the United States and having certain privileges would give me advantages in access and range that could be used to their benefit. And so I came back to California and I stayed.

Shortly after I returned to the Bay Area, Chile suffered the coup that resulted in Salvador Allende's assassination and the rise of General Pinochet. The work that we had started with the people of Central America and El Salvador was thus combined with work related to Chile, because there were many people disappeared all throughout Latin America during these years. We opened a human rights office for political prisoners and the disappeared. I had to help manage campaigns designed to help find important disappeared individuals, which is one of the most beautiful things I have ever had to do. There I worked closely with religious leaders, working-class representatives, students, medical professionals and others who were engaged in our evolving human rights activities.

The first case that I had was that of Ricardo Calderón, dean of the University of El Salvador. They had him in Mariona. He was a political challenge to the authorities for having wanted to raise his employees' salaries against the counsel of government education officials. So they were mistreating him, hurting him physically. His wife was very worried because she feared that he would be killed. I had recently met some people whom I trusted and who could support me in organizing a delegation to visit El Salvador and inquire about the dean's circumstances. So we empanelled a delegation with a congressman, a physician, a nurse, a nun and a member of the growing Solidarity Movement in El Salvador with whom I communicated. It was incredible that we were able to mount the campaign. The participating organizations were barely starting. Our early efforts laid the groundwork for how we would effectively function in later years. Public response to our delegation project was so favorable in the United States that we were able to coordinate with officials in Washington to pressure members of congress in El Salvador. The campaign went well. Many impressive people were involved and all of us learned important lessons about the power of organizing for basic democratic rights. We learned that being in solidarity with others is truly to give something of oneself in order to gain something vital in return. Too many people think that human rights work and politics is something mechanical, something that only benefits a minority or special interest of which they are often not a member. People typically fail to see how this work also benefits them, indeed *all* of us.

During the campaign to free Calderón, we educated people in the United States about El Salvador. We explained to them who the prisoner was and why he was detained. People here became especially interested because Calderón was dean of a university. They knew that he was admired by the students and his professional colleagues. To the average American the idea of such a person being subjected to an indefinite jail sentence absent formal charges spoke to something being fundamentally wrong in El Salvador.

We emphasized the severity of Calderón's plight by naming the crime against him as torture. To many Americans, this was initially discomforting if off-putting. There were indeed people who would get upset and not tolerate hearing the word "torture." And then, finally, once past their defensiveness and disbelief, they would ask why this was happening. When we clarified the conditions facing the people, we gained quick support. Many people came out, and Ricardo Calderón became a symbol for the entire community in support of solidarity. Our delegation did not give up and, after a difficult but well-thought-out campaign, we succeeded in freeing Ricardo Calderón.

As our work evolved, people in the Solidarity Movement started learning about the economic and political systems that were manifestly creating injustice in El Salvador and surrounding nations. We wanted and needed to be informed and concrete, rather than overly theoretical and naïve as we reached out for additional public and official support. At the same time, as we pursued our work focused on circumstances in Central America, we began to build our institutional base of resistance here in the United States. This involved the care and feeding of important domestic organizations and networks in support of the Solidarity Movement south of the U.S. border.

In 1975, Casa El Salvador and a small newspaper called *El Pulgarcito* started, and I participated in those efforts because, like my activist counterparts in El Salvador, I felt that if we were well organized internationally we could do even more. Soon thereafter, the Casa Farabundo Martí was formed. Although it did not yet specialize in social justice activism as such, it served from the beginning to address all the human and social needs of Solidarity here in the Bay Area. By the early- to mid-1980s, other organizations—generally more avowedly activist in nature—started forming to fill evolving and unmet needs related to the growing problems in El Salvador. That is when CRECEN, the Comité de Refugiados, was born in San Francisco. CARECEN, the allied network of Central American refugee and resource centers that emerged in Houston, Los Angeles, New York and Washington, DC, formed during this period as well.

In CRECEN, I was responsible for working with women. There were many women who fought in El Salvador. Among those who had taken up arms and been injured was a cohort that came to the United States as refugees. With these women, we started a work unit to clean houses, so that they could earn money. They had to learn everything: what liquids to use with what and where, how to clean perfectly, how to charge their clients. We taught and advised on all of these concerns as we supported these women's transitions. We also succeeded in getting support from North Americans, and especially great support from Anglo women, to teach the Salvadorans how to use computers. If we had a fundraiser, our Anglo women benefactors would always come to help. They would translate, and we soon started a bilingual solidarity exchange.

CRECEN's work was increasingly comprehensive. There was much going on besides the jobs creation and training work that I was involved in shaping. We also had a mental health group where some of the women would speak about their experiences in the war, with the men and how it was that they became involved. Some, it turned out, got involved unknowingly, based on lies and misinformation that they had received from the men around them. We then started an organization called El Salvador Today, NEST, to create sister cities relationships that could help us to further solidarity. In this way, from the United States, we could send people to dig wells, or teachers, doctors and professionals who could teach people in key skill areas while providing them with moral support as well.

Several sisterhoods were established in El Salvador and the United States; some are still active today. One example of this is located in San Antonio de los Ranchos, which to the best of my knowledge is still a sister city of Verti, California. The Sanctuaries also created sisterhoods and the local Sanctuary; South Bay Sanctuary started working near Lempa River. I think they still work in Segundo Montes and in another nearby community. And they continue on and on. Aline Shaw is the director of the American group that travels to El Salvador twice each year. They have taught the Salvadorans how to harvest soy. They are well organized. Their Salvadoran women counterparts are also typically well organized. They have committees that control their respective regions. They have very nice chicken coops; they have water wells and good education programs. People who travel from here, particularly to that place, are customarily older people. Elderly people in the United States are very strong and dedicated. Some of them visited El Salvador for the first time in 1984 in a caravan of several buses. Those people have been very constant for me. Beyond their contributions to the solidarity and sanctuary struggles, they have worked hard for the people of El Salvador on other humanitarian fronts as well, such as in the aftermath of a great flood that afflicted the area in conjunction with Hurricane Mitch a few years ago.

Around the time that Hurricane Mitch struck the region, the SHARE Foundation got started. It has had strong support from the religious sector and from women. SHARE believes that the war did not solve El Salvador's problems, in truth, since there are still overwhelming numbers of poor people in that country who need fundamental assistance and change. SHARE has the idea that we should support the poor by constructing collective communities that harvest honey or make orange juice in La Libertad and other places. So they have continued with the work of solidarity, taking on the basic and human needs of the Salvadoran people; and they are essentially doing this without taking into consideration what the government says. They are growing a parallel society that functions in another way; I think that is very healthy. SHARE's approach acknowledges that the economic situation has not fundamentally changed in El Salvador and that people have to survive in some way or another. It offers a dynamic alternative to conventional development policies.

CARECEN is also one of the great organizations that has been able—speaking of human rights—to respond to the Salvadoran people's needs in the United States: immigration advocacy, mental and physical health support, coexistence strategy—all of these things are critically important to keep the refugee population here informed and moving forward. As a result of this work, Salvadorans throughout the Bay Area and the nation are always on top of what is happening in their home country; they are always available to send help when needed, like they did when the devastation of Hurricane Mitch struck. I do not know how many thousands of dollars were sent, but the support was considerable. Salvadorans are always ready to help when any major event occurs in El Salvador or here that affects the community and its needs.

My memories of the struggle for justice both here and in El Salvador are many and profound. Another thing that I remember from the past involving CARECEN, for example, was that Ramón Cardona, one its principals, was kidnapped in Honduras. They detained him and were planning to disappear him. I was working in San Francisco with the press agency, Sal Press of El Salvador, and each night, at around 11 pm, I would always get a call from Mexico with news updates. I would record the news and exchange briefly with my Mexican news associates. As I was listening to the news on this particular night, taking notes, I heard that Ramón Cardona had disappeared at the Honduras airport, and the first thing that came to my mind was "Who is Ramón Cardona?" I then realized he was an important leader of the Salvadoran Solidarity Movement with strong connections to the Bay Area.

The following day, very early in the morning, a group of us met, accordingly, to organize a campaign to get Ramón out of captivity. We had to do this in a hurry. It was not clear that we would be able to have the same success in this case as we had with Ricardo Calderón earlier. Father Moriarti who had a church in what is now the Castro District, The Holy Redeemer Church, supported our efforts. He let us sleep in rooms that he had available there, for free. I stayed there for most of Ramón's campaign, making phone calls, etc. From the church, we organized a delegation that as always, included people from Solidarity, a relative of Ramón, some lawyers, a doctor and a nun. It was hard because those who held Ramón did not want to release him and they were considered sufficiently dangerous that the U.S. State Department discouraged our delegation from traveling to Honduras to seek his freedom. Eventually, after great effort and additional support from some key members of the U.S. Congress, we succeeded in convincing Ramón's captors to release him, and a delegation went to Honduras and brought him back. He had been placed in a metal box outside of the designated pick-up point. His abduction was a serious matter, to be sure.

Around this time, many Salvadoran refugees started to arrive in cities and towns all throughout the northern California region, from San Jose to San Francisco. I had begun to work closely again with Catholic Charities. As the number of Salvadoran refugees coming into our region to get out of harm's way began to mount, Catholic Charities secured support to start a mental health clinic for people traumatized by the war and especially for those who were tortured. In San Francisco, psychologists started an allied anti-torture organization. I got involved because I loved people and I thought that the worst that could happen to anyone ever was being subject to official torture. I had also studied psychology. We named the organization Olin—the Mayan symbol of eternal change. By that time, people from the United Nations came to investigate. In El Salvador, a truth commission was established to surface the extent and specifics of the now more than decade-long fundamental violations of human rights that had been taking hold there. I and many of my colleagues in San Francisco interviewed refugees who had been victims of torture and persecution. We interviewed all kinds of people: soldiers, civilians, women, men and even children.

There was one young man whom I interviewed that I will never forget. He started out with the Atlacatal Battalion. The young man was very bad off when I met him and he told me his sad story. When he was fifteen, he was hanging out with a group of other young men playing basketball at school. The battalion showed up and took all of them. That is when things started down a dark path for him. He reviewed the process of how they were trained. Through a series of physical and mental challenges, the officers would press the soldiers to the limits of their capacities. He revealed that few of those who were in the battalions were there because they wanted to be. Most, like him, were taken by force, involuntarily. He also told me that he was forced at gun point to torture a girl in Huazapan and to do barbaric things to her at the request of his commanding officers. The girl, it turns out, was suspected of being a low level operative of an anti-government protest network. These experiences had made the ex-soldier not well, both physically and emotionally.

Like the sad soldier from the Atlacatal Battalion, there were many others I had the opportunity and responsibility to interview in order to advance the work of the Truth Commission. I spent two or three years doing this work and, to be entirely honest, I had to get out because after a time I just could not take it anymore. It was making me neurotic to learn of all the horrible things that had happened during the war years. The beautiful and redeeming thing was to see how most people recovered with time, at least in terms of their will and ability to move on, despite the worst of what had happened in the past.

Olin still exists. It is run by a Salvadoran doctor. It supports a dentist, a doctor and various psychologists. In El Salvador, the same kind of support networks were created and still live on as well. In fact, it is important to note that in many cases the Salvadoran patients and psychologists who have exchanged with American professionals on the issues have been able to teach our best about effective intervention therapies that had not been thought of here before. The injuries sustained were brutal as in any war, but in El Salvador a large part of the equation lies with the especially disturbing realization that fellow countrymen inflicted these wounds on the people.

The permanence of wounds incurred under these circumstances, whether physical or emotional, is particularly profound. To lose an arm or a leg is hard enough. To lose your nation and your sense of identity as a result of a devastating civil war, as many refugees were forced to is still another level of loss. The injuries that many sustained will remain with them for the rest of their lives. One female compatriot I met along the way is a living example of this. She had a bullet lodged in her head. The operating physicians could not take it out without killing her. It is now a part of her forever, wherever she goes, whatever she does.

This sort of permanent sacrifice and suffering is very sad when you consider that only a small minority of people involved participated in the popular movement because they had an ideological fight to wage. The majority of those killed, injured or displaced during the war were very poor people. They merely wanted to better their own and their family's living conditions. What they wanted was a just and safe country. Fundamentally, they did not want new cars, cellular phones or houses. Nor were most preoccupied with revolutionary or other political theories as such. They simply wanted justice, basic human rights, and they were very clear about that.

When the peace treaties were signed by leaders of the competing camps in 1992, the poor and the victims, the *campesinos* of the El Salvador war, also became part of the process because they were promised lands and a series of other benefits under the accords. When they made demands of the new government, accordingly, to fulfill all that had been agreed on, the government simply did not respond. Then, unexpectedly, an alliance was struck between the *campesinos* and the young men who fought in the military and were also crippled or otherwise disabled. Together, the two groups discovered they shared some of the same interests and they decided to fight for their rights collectively. In time, they began to include women as leaders in their cause; there were many crippled women, too. These alliances appear to have resulted in some brief socioeconomic improvements following the war's conclusion; but more recent evidence suggests that too little has changed for the disadvantaged in El Salvador in recent years.

One of the saddest legacies of the war experience in my opinion is the continuing distrust and discord that exists in still too many relationships between Salvadorans who were directly involved in the conflicts of the 1980s and 1990s. I learned about all of this after 1993 when I began receiving groups of mostly female Salvadoran refugee leaders as they came to the United States to take classes. They impressed me with their honest, unassuming and straightforward thought. They were not confused; they knew what had happened. But as the months and years passed, one began to see people in the former Solidarity Movement arguing with each other. I found the conflict and the bickering very confusing and unnecessary. People would argue largely over personal issues; but in the end it was all about unresolved political issues that burned within them despite a radical change in the immediate circumstances they faced. They had all experienced massive changes and loss during the prior ten years; they had suffered a lot and did not have the tools to manage it well much of the time.

With the passage of time, I would say that community advocates in El Salvador are probably doing better overall nowadays, in the sense that their organizations have legal standing. They are recognized by the government as a result of strong public organizing after the war, including several major demonstrations during those initial years when they continued to be repressed. Because of these struggles, they now have several important model projects taking shape in the San Vicente area, El Paisnal. Presently, I am working on such a project. It seeks to promote hydroponics as a vehicle for women's economic development in the region.

Hydroponics involves cultivating food using nutrient-enriched water immersion techniques. It is essentially aquaculture. For the people of El Salvador, it is a new way of planting and harvesting. Right now, they are growing radishes, lettuces, carrots and watercress with this method with increasing success. The technique is highly accessible to people in a nation like El Salvador. It is a low cost undertaking that can take place initially in a space as small as one's home. You start the seed and when it is ready to be planted, you transfer it. You can coordinate different foods based on their varying harvest cycles: radishes will take until November; lettuce will be sold in two months, and so forth. Using the technique this way, the participating women have great dual advantages. In essence, hydroponics meets both their immediate need for affordable food for their families, as well as their associated need for increased family income, since they can both consume and sell these products.

Another example of renewed civic vitality in El Salvador is Médicos Solidarios, or Solidarity Doctors. When the conflict with social security and the cost of medicine was going on a few years back, Médicos Solidarios came out and gave medicine to people outside of the hospitals. They also took up a very public fight for more socialized medical cost management with the government by insisting that medical services should not be thought of as a commodity, but rather as a human right. While medical costs are still an issue in El Salvador, as here in the United States, the very capacity of a group like Médicos Solidarios to effectively challenge the government on these issues suggests that El Salvador's governance is evolving. In more recent times, Médicos Solidarios has developed very interesting projects designed to expand access to care for El Salvador's poor and needy. Most interesting perhaps, they have started a promising partnership with Fundelidi, an organization for the disabled, to manufacture portable chairs for dental and other medical procedures targeted to the physically impaired.

As I reflect back on my experiences related to El Salvador, I want to say in closing that my nuclear family was an important part of my participation in the Solidarity Movement. My husband during those years was a Sandinista, and the Sandinistas had established relationships with important supporters in California as early as 1981. At the time, our son was very little but I would nevertheless take him along when I would attend political meetings related to the Central American struggles. I was beginning to host groups of Salvadoran women at that time, and I wanted very much to show these other women that they should not think that the only situation in which a woman can have a child is the comfort of a home. I wanted them to see that they could be loving mothers and be involved in social justice work. Therefore, I would take my son almost anywhere that my organizing work took me in those days. As a result, I became involved in many things that dealt with children and, since I have considerable professional experience as a teacher, I was very interested in good education and healthy kids.

The matter of how we relate to our children, especially about the kind of experiences I recount here, is a sensitive one. Several years after my son was born and my then-husband and I had continued to work hard for the struggle, I decided that I should pay more attention to our son. I felt that something was not right, something that I had not noticed before—not only for my son, but for young people in general. I was, and am, convinced that consciousness forms at a very early age and provides children with the capacity to see things that allow them in many cases to have no barriers. So in more recent years I have returned to teaching and working mainly with young people. Sadly, except in only indirect ways, this has diminished my daily connection with El Salvador and all the history that I have shared in this interview.

The last time that I went to El Salvador, in fact, was during the elections of 1994. I went with a group to keep watch, and I wrote a very interesting report on it. In reality there were no meaningful elections. It was all merely a farce to deceive the people. During that trip, I met my current husband through an Argentinean artist who was part of the delegation I organized. He (my husband) is from Chalchuapal. At the time of our meeting, he was at Ciudad Delgado making art with his press. Because I am also an artist—I paint, write, play music and make jewelry, and because art was a large part of my life before I became involved in politics, our meeting was profoundly meaningful to me. But another factor made our meeting especially significant and bonding; namely, it turned out that when I met this new love of my life in El Salvador, my mother passed away.

When my mother died, I faced the most uncertain hours of my life. I needed something to help me find my peace with it. I thus spent some time making art with my new husband-to-be and that turned out to be an incredible therapy for me. In the countryside of El Salvador, I could feel my mother everywhere—in the thunder and the rain, in all of the surrounding soil, in the plants and all that. That sensation of her presence proved remarkably healing to me. When I returned to the United States, I decided not to dedicate twenty-four hours a day to Sanctuary, as I had for most of my adult life over the prior decade. I think one starts realizing with time that there are other things that demand one's focus in the course of a life, things that are not merely political or intellectual in nature, but rather informed by a sense of spirituality and art. I felt that I could no longer function at the speed required by social justice movement work, nor did I want to anymore.

I have a great comfort in knowing that I did everything within my power to stand for peace and justice during my younger years. I believe that my generation of Salvadoran American leaders made a difference and created an important space for subsequent gains, both here in the United States and in El Salvador. In those days, we worked all hours of the day, every day for the cause. We did what we had to do. I have no regrets; but neither do I live under any illusions. I still believe in peace and justice. But I have a very different relationship nowadays to time and the world of politics. What I like now is to treat each aspect of my life with great care and concentration—to do one thing at a time, rather than ten.

Isabel Beltrán

My name is Isabel Beltrán Orantes and I am from San Salvador, El Salvador. My early memories are filled with trauma. When I was a little girl, my father suffered a serious accident. A wood beam fell from the second floor of a home he was helping to build and it hit him. He was seriously injured. My mother had an accident around this same time too, though less serious than my father's; a piece of iron got stuck in her foot. Me and my siblings were all very small when these things happened. It was terrifying for us. I remember that my father had to be hospitalized for a long time. That affected me a lot because all my memories of that time are of him lying in bed.

On account of my father's injuries, our family had no bread winner for many months. All of us children were very young at the time, too young to get employment, and my mother was also unable to work during this period because of her injury. With no one in our family able to work, we faced a big problem. Unsettling memories from this early part of my childhood have stayed with me. Even now, when I pass by a construction site, I walk away right away. It is like an unhealed wound. Though I have experienced less and less discomfort with it all in recent years, these childhood stresses affected me a lot. I have a large family: eight siblings. Altogether, we are five females and four males. Seven of us now live in the United States. My other two siblings are in El Salvador. As large as our family is, it could have been even larger. In fact, my mother had twelve children, but three passed away during infancy or early childhood.

I left El Salvador long before the war was in full force. I came to the United States in 1975. At that time, the early conflicts leading to the war that raged through the 1980s were beginning. I was mostly uninvolved politically at that time, although I did participate in some light resistance activities in El Salvador before I left for the States. I immigrated not so much because of the war, although I did lose three of my friends to the conflict before I emigrated. I was certainly aware of the growing problems that were creating more violence all around us. At the time, however, the evidence of this growing conflict was still relatively subtle. In relation to leaving El Salvador for the United States, I was more concerned about giving my family a better life. I wanted to gain educational and work opportunities in the United States that could help my family members back home.

The war definitely gave me a helpful push to leave my country; it helped me to overcome the fear I felt in pursuing a life so far away from what I knew, so that I could indeed help my family economically and facilitate a better life for all of us. Without much planning or preparation, I thus made arrangements to relocate to Los Angeles. I remember that I only had one acquaintance in California at the time. In essence, I came to the United States without knowing anyone. It was really hard to come here from El Salvador without a more solid tie to this country. I was really on my own and I had no idea what sort of life I would find here. The one acquaintance I knew in California cleaned a house for a living but did not have an apartment. This meant that I had nowhere to stay upon my arrival, which made for a very anxious beginning. I had to hide at the house where my friend cleaned for about five days, until we were able to leave that house and find a more permanent home.

While we looked for housing, my friend took me to various work agencies so I could find a job. I took the first job offered to me. I only lasted a week. The job required me to walk and take care of more than one dozen dogs. I had never done anything like that, and at the time I did not know how to speak English. All of this made for complications in my ability to succeed in my first job here. The dog owners who hired me were wealthy people. Their expectations were very high and they were unable to be patient with me. A big part of the problem was communication. I did not know basic things and I could not effectively communicate with them. It was frustrating for all of us. After just a few days, I honestly could not handle it anymore. I found another job and then another. I cleaned houses because that was one of the few things that I knew how to do and that did not require a lot of language skills or client contact; my friend did the same thing.

Particularly because I came to the United States not knowing English and not having a profession, I was faced with immediate culture shock and I did not really have anyone here to help me through it. It was a very lonely journey for me. At that time, El Salvador was largely an unknown land among most North Americans. There was only a tiny community of Salvadorans here at the time and it was highly dispersed throughout the region. There was still relatively little news coverage of events taking shape in El Salvador. People like me were effectively invisible in and unfamiliar to the larger North American culture.

In this situation, I focused on survival and I somehow stumbled through the next several years without any major negative incidents. Slowly but surely I learned English and I became more comfortable with my life here and my surroundings. One day in 1979, I received an invitation to participate at the upcoming meeting of a local Central American committee. I did not know anyone associated with this group and so I did not attend the gathering; but I was intrigued to learn that such a committee existed. I found myself wondering what they were trying to achieve, what kinds of activities and events they organized. I thought the group was mainly dedicated to cultural activities. Though it seems strange to say it now, I actually was entirely naïve about the situation that my country was beginning to experience by 1979. No one at home or elsewhere had told me anything about the extent to which El Salvador was becoming enmeshed in civil war, or about the associated atrocities that were beginning to occur *en masse*. I had not read of any of this in newspapers, nor seen anything on television.

Information about the growing conflict in El Salvador was not yet being widely disseminated to people living in the United States. American journalists and human rights groups were only just then beginning to learn about the situation. My access to information about the conflict through loved ones back home was unwittingly limited by my family's reluctance to say anything to me about it, out of fear that doing so would subject all of us to violent retaliation. I only learned about this years later.

In 1980, I met someone involved in the Comité Farabundo Martí, which was then beginning to report on circumstances in El Salvador, here in the United States. I was invited to attend a meeting and I went without thinking much about it. What I learned there encouraged me to become more involved. I started to meet and work regularly with the committee. A large part of our work involved gathering and disseminating information about events taking shape in El Salvador. Our goal was to educate U.S.-based and other international audiences about the repressive policies and state-supported atrocities that were beginning to emerge from El Salvador. We wanted in this way to encourage protests and interventions that might help put an end to the worst of what was happening in my country. That motivated me.

Over the next decade, I became more and more involved in this work. I had always intuitively had the desire to be a part of fighting for justice, especially in my country. I knew from my own life experiences that there were many problems facing our people, especially the poor, and that there existed organizations committed to this work. I also knew that people who had organized and advocated for these things in El Salvador had been persecuted for wanting better things for our people and it made me angry. So I got involved little by little, until by the late 1980s I was completely drawn in. At that time, I started working full time in community organizing and advocacy.

During the decade leading up to my full time engagement in social justice work, many people began to flee El Salvador. Most started arriving in the United States and I became increasingly involved in efforts to help them adjust to life in this country. I worked with the Solidarity Movement from its incipiency. I got involved in everything. My largest contribution was coordinating a project to attract North American support, to help Americans, Canadians and others see what was going on in El Salvador. That is how I started taking on responsibilities within the movement. In addition, although I was not directly involved with the Sanctuary Movement that was also very active at this time, I always coordinated projects with leaders of Sanctuary wherever that was possible. Our combined efforts were increasingly important and powerful levers to manage and then ultimately end the conflict in El Salvador during these years. At this time, we were all advancing a lot of resistance activities, such as hunger strikes and peace marches. I became involved in all of this work.

I especially remember one protest march that we organized through the Comité Farabundo Martí and other groups in downtown Los Angeles. I remember there were several hundred of us on the streets marching peacefully and that we were nevertheless met by surprising police repression. Many of the attending officers were on horseback. At a certain point, they charged their large horses toward us. People were injured and frightened. Despite intimidation and other setbacks of this sort, we forged ahead. People exhibited a great deal of courage in these moments. We were all motivated by a deep belief in our cause.

I remember participating in a lot of protest events in San Francisco during this period. San Francisco hosted some of the largest solidarity events in the United States, so we would always travel from Los Angeles to participate in them. We would go in buses, taking large numbers of protestors and providing support for them all along the way. I participated in a lot of these events because I thought it was important for all of us in the movement, wherever we might sit geographically, to work together. At that time, in southern California, the Comité Farabundo Martí had a steady organizing group of more than 350 Salvadorans, who could be counted on to support marches and public education projects designed to inform people who wanted to know about what was going in El Salvador. We did a lot of things to increase public awareness of the issues and to support popular response mobilizations.

I remember that we organized Tamaleadas (tamale sales) to raise funds for the Comité's activities during these times. We would gather in a house to make the tamales, and then go sell them in various neighborhoods and communities. We would take literature on El Salvador along with us, so that people could be informed in writing about what was happening. We remained very busy and active throughout this entire period of time, and we worked closely and effectively with many other peace and justice organizations that had formed to promote reform in El Salvador; so, we promoted movement unity work as well.

Eventually, as part of this work, we began to organize film viewings to showcase events or issues related to El Salvador. One time we showed a film in the Fiesta Theater. It played over a weekend, from

Friday evening through Sunday afternoon. We filled the theatre at every showing. People were desperate for information. By this time, the Salvadoran population had begun to grow rapidly in southern California. Between 1980 and 1982, there was a huge immigration upswing among Salvadorans, most of them refugees seeking relief from the violence and atrocities beginning to come out of El Salvador. As a result, the Solidarity Movement was growing bigger by the month. We would organize more and more enormous events at important venues during this time; and each time we would fill them. As we pursued this work, we also began to gain essential support from North American allies who wanted to help us. By supporting our efforts with increasing contributions of money, talent and time, they expressed their solidarity with us.

My role in the movement changed several times over the years, but in each instance I remained fundamentally committed to the cause of peace and justice for the Salvadoran people. As a paid community organizer, I first worked with the Comité de Refugiados Centroamericanos (the Central American Refugee Committee). There I had a very active role; I earned the respect of the people, as well as their trust. The Comité played an important role in the founding of CARECEN, the Central American Resource Center, which in subsequent years went on to become one of the United States' premier refugee rights organizations. The Comité's leaders wanted to support the development of a new institution that could provide direct assistance to undocumented Salvadorans. These Salvadoran émigrés to the United States were mired in challenges ranging from gaining legal consideration as protected international refugees to securing housing, jobs and needed medical treatment.

CARECEN was established to provide an organized response capacity to these many pressing needs. I went to work at CARECEN following its establishment in Los Angeles and I stayed there for many years as a program coordinator. During the war, I was particularly involved in the creation of an inspiring solidarity project—a sister cities program that linked Los Angeles and other U.S. urban centers to various Salvadoran cities and towns. Through this work, we created many successful sisterhoods and took delegations of North Americans to see firsthand the situation in El Salvador. We thus took many North Americans on tours of El Salvador during the war, which was a very difficult thing to do.

For those of us who were Salvadorans returning to our country of origin as progressives against the government's policies, we exposed ourselves through this work to the worst kind of retaliation. In addition, our North American guests were ultimately subject to the inherent dangers of El Salvador's growing internal conflict, something over which we had relatively little if any control. Overall, these considerable risks proved worth taking. While we did experience frequent challenges and even real dangers, we were mainly able to expose our North American allies to El Salvador's darkest realities during this time in ways that enabled them to return to the United States with information and convictions even more supportive of our cause than would have been otherwise possible.

This was work that I really enjoyed because, aside from raising awareness about El Salvador's growing political problems, we helped many communities of our brothers and sisters there by providing aid to youth and other needy groups affected by the war. In one community, we built a nursery; in another, we contributed to the local elementary school. At a regional level, we built a new school in Illacurilla. That was a particularly powerful experience. The surrounding community had recently been badly affected by the conflict. When we got to Illacurilla, we could see lingering signs of the Sumpul massacre in which countless innocent peasants had been killed by reactionary, pro-government forces. I remember that local leaders took us to a mill where a family went to seek refuge thinking they would be safe. To our collective shock and horror, what we found when we arrived at the mill were remnants of brains and blood all over the walls. It was a disturbing sight that simultaneously sickened me and motivated me to continue my deepening involvement in social justice work.

I think I was able to help the movement a lot during this time. Through my involvement in the Comité Farabundo Martí, I was able to help facilitate CARECEN's early start and success. The Comité's initial funding of CARECEN and our early collaboration with their leaders, really helped to anchor the Salvadoran refugee community in ways that we could not even appreciate at the time. Our two organizations worked very closely as a team during this period, and I was personally active in this work for many years.

When CARECEN began operations, it lacked everything. People who worked at CARECEN during that time did so for little or no pay; they did it out of love. I also worked as a volunteer health promoter for them back then and I organized a medical clinic for the community, which was quite small. Pro bono doctors would come by once every week to provide free medical services to needy community members. We had almost no support resources to offer our medical volunteers. We were so poor, in fact, that whenever women had to have a pap exam, we would simply place a sheet over an office desk and our physicians would use that as a medical table.

I also worked with CARECEN and a sister organization then known as CRECEN to raise funds for new organizations and initiatives and to create public educational exchange opportunities to underscore how violence and repression were resulting from U.S. and Salvadoran government policies in Central America. I then worked for two years as the coordinator of another organization that provided public information from El Salvador. We sponsored various leading Salvadoran scholars to present to North American university audiences on the issues and were met by huge crowds of interested intellectuals, students and media organizations on each occasion. Much of that sort of work helped to advance everything that we were able to accomplish and build as a community in subsequent years.

The formation of CARECEN was especially important at this time. CARECEN was principally a grassroots service organization that was initially formed to represent the interests of Salvadoran newcomers in the U.S. social welfare system. But in time its role expanded to assist the many Salvadoran refugees who had no legal representation to secure legal protected status through which they could remain and work in the United States. It is important to recall that many Salvadorans who came to the United States during this time were quickly incarcerated as illegal aliens. Despite their claims to asylum protection, the U.S. official policy of that time refused to recognize Salvadoran émigrés as political refugees. In response to these circumstances, CARECEN began working with Sanctuary Movement leaders to prevent Salvadorans from being returned to El Salvador where they might be tortured or killed out of retaliation for their past political dissent or their attempt to seek exile abroad. So, during this early period, CARECEN became an institution that provided legal aid to Salvadoran asylum seekers who were already here, as well as to those who had only recently arrived and who had access to no other form of legal assistance.

The quest to achieve U.S. governmental recognition of our community's largely refugee composition was a huge struggle that we fought hard for. In time, we finally achieved this recognition. Our victory was the result of a large movement of Salvadorans and North Americans who came together to take our case to the U.S. Congress. Once the Congress recognized the conflict in El Salvador to be a civil war, rather than an outside-influenced insurgency (as the Reagan administration had always claimed) it had to give affected Salvadorans an opportunity to obtain political asylum. CARECEN played an important role in this process, representing refugees who were fleeing the war to escape torture and death. Owing largely to this legacy, many of my friends and colleagues have worked with CARECEN since its incipiency. Still today, CARECEN must be regarded as one of our community's most vital and essential institutions. Its work was crucial then as our community formed here in the United States; and, though we have moved forward in many respects, the organization's work remains very important to our community today.

Looking back on it all, I think the work we did in the 1980s and 1990s as new participants in American civic culture was significant and enduring. For those of us who were centrally involved in this work, we experienced long years of struggle and hardship. We had to endure and escape the war. We had to fight for official acknowledgment of the civil war in our nation, as well as our legitimate status as international refugees with all of the rights corresponding to that. Despite the many challenges we faced, we achieved many important things because we worked hard, organized effectively at the grassroots level, engaged with important North American supporters and lobbied strongly at an institutional level in the U.S. Congress.

Though it took too long, our community organizing efforts ultimately helped to stop the war and the killing in El Salvador, as well as across much of Central America. This is a large accomplishment considering the millions and millions of dollars in foreign aid funding that were provided by North American authorities to El Salvador during the Reagan administration—funding that largely supported terror against the Salvadoran people by our own government. Salvadoran community members like me would not have rejected that aid had it been directed to social programs intended to help El Salvador get ahead, or to support development of the country. But, sadly, in the name of North American people, those resources were used instead to destroy liberties, to purchase armaments, to train death squads, to kill and torture people, etc. Our efforts ultimately halted these thoughtless and illegal activities.

The other achievement that I am proud of is the temporary work permit that our movement helped to establish as a legitimate instrument of U.S. immigration policy in times of regional political unrest that produce large numbers of asylum applicants requiring at least temporary refuge in North America. We were the first American refugee population to obtain temporary work permits (TPS) for the asylum applicants who came here from El Salvador during the 1980s. Since our victory in this connection, other at-risk refugee groups, including Guatemalans, have benefited from this innovation in legal rights and protection for asylum applicants.

We had to fight very hard for the TPS designation. Indeed, we had to organize ourselves as never before. The fight for TPS informed our first ever nationwide effort to gather signatures to establish broad public support for our aims. Neither the Salvadoran nor the Guatemalan communities carried a lot of weight in Congress at this time, so our first step was to send a lot of letters to leading elected members of Congress during 1986 and 1987 to ground our claims. We organized caravans of Salvadorans throughout the country to support rallies and public education campaigns. Our campaign banner read: "*Ningún ser humano es ilegal*" (No human being is illegal). I think I still have a copy of that poster. I helped to organize important elements of that campaign and I am proud to this day of what we were able to accomplish. We visited seventy-five cities and twenty-five states. We went to schools, colleges, universities and congress people's offices—everywhere and anywhere that would get us needed support to gain a special temporary protected status under U.S. and international law.

Our caravans departed from Los Angeles, New York and other major cities with large Salvadoran and Central American populations. Their common destination was Washington, DC, where we planned to descend upon Congress to plead our case. It was a big struggle to get all but the most progressive congressmembers to support our cause. We had to regroup and initiate several more major surges in organizational and political initiative over the coming years to succeed in relation to TPS. Ultimately, we did succeed, though, with the help of other organizations, supportive North American institutional leaders and a handful of leading congressional representatives who helped us work through the complicated structures of U.S. policy formation.

Looking back on our experience and ultimate success in connection with the TPS, it is sometimes hard to believe how we prevailed. We were so poor. In that first caravan trip from Los Angeles to Washington, we did not even have a car secured to make the journey when we announced the project. So someone had to donate a van that we ended up using as our principal vehicle. It was an un-upholstered ramshackle. Driving in that van, I will never forget when we would get to places where it was snowing or raining en route to Washington. We would literally have to cover our heads with blankets because the water would leak into the passenger cabin as we drove.

Ironically, I did not make it all the way to Washington to complete the first TPS advocacy campaign in Congress. Along the way, I received a call informing me that Salvadorans were being repatriated from Honduras to Colomencahue. The situation presented real risks for the repatriated Salvadorans back in El Salvador—risks of reprisal ranging from torture to mass murder at the hands of Salvadoran government authorities or vigilante groups. News of the Honduran repatriation required me urgently to return to Los Angeles where I would be better positioned to assist our constituents affected by the new developments in Honduras.

In time, our hard work paid off. We secured TPS designations for many of our people and also paved the way for a cessation of the worst of U.S. and Salvadoran governmental over-reaching in El Salvador. We also facilitated the establishment of an important new national community of Salvadorans in this country through the formation of effective and responsive civic and support organizations—

organizations that have helped both Salvadorans and others to benefit from our community's growing presence in the United States. For someone like me who was heavily involved in this work, all of these accomplishments make you value what we have done. For example, CARECEN is now a nationally recognized institution that continues to work with people in our community. They have a large continuing responsibility, but one built on a sound and impressive legacy. People like me who played a role in advancing this work left our seeds there, and those seeds have blossomed. To think of this makes me happy because I do see the results. It makes me realize that all that work me and others did at the beginning was worthwhile.

Now we have a different community. We are no longer refugees. One sees Salvadorans everywhere who have overcome many barriers. We are experiencing more and more success in important areas, such as education, business and politics. We have contributed substantially to this country at all levels: economic, cultural, political and otherwise. From all of this it is safe to say that Salvadorans are here to stay now, and that we are an increasingly important element of North American culture.

Today, I remain active in the community, though not as much as I was when we began to organize more than twenty years ago. I now work at SALEF, El Fondo Salvadoreño Americano por el Liderazgo y la Educación (the Salvadoran American Leadership and Educational Fund). SALEF promotes leadership education for emerging Salvadoran community leaders and, in the process, directly engages them in dialogues and projects with important California elected and appointed officials, business leaders, foundation executives and other state opinion leaders. They give scholarships to low-income students and they help undocumented youths with skills training so that they can become leaders wherever they may live, work or study. I have been working there since 2004. I started with a technology project that SALEF sponsors in the Pico-Union District of Los Angeles, where we do computer training among other activities. I have also been involved in coordinating an allied project that helps interested Salvadoran community members to become certified by the state to work in medical offices.

I never imagined that I would work with SALEF because, in the past, the majority of their programs were for youth. But, in time, as the community's needs have evolved, SALEF has expanded its focus to include more mid-career oriented constituencies, in addition to younger and emerging professionals. The technology project I helped to establish in Pico-Union was a program for adults from its incipiency. Since I am older now, adults can easily identify with me. I really like my job. It enables me to continue working in the community; I thus continue to do my part.

At SALEF I continue to focus on responding to Salvadoran community needs. I am presently taking nutrition classes because I want to help our community in that aspect too; there is hardly any information available on nutrition that targets Salvadorans, and especially our younger community members. It is important that I am presently affiliated with an organization that is principally concerned with young people. As established leaders like me get older and sustaining our vitality becomes an issue, it is essential to have young people involved in the business of shaping our community's future. We need to cultivate youth who have an interest in community affairs and who are aware of the larger dynamics shaping our times. This is increasingly difficult to do, since so many of our young people today no longer seem to have the same desire to help. There is no war in El Salvador, we are established here, children are in school, we face seemingly less pressing needs. And yet our work is far from done. There are many of our people here as well as back in El Salvador who have continuing unmet needs because the fundamental problems in society have not relented, even if for the time being they have become less visible on the surface than when people like me first came to this country. Poverty and injustice, for example, still sadly exist here and in El Salvador, and life remains very difficult, therefore, for too many people in both nations.

Largely on account of continuing social and economic hardships, our people continue to immigrate to the United States. They continue to leave El Salvador, not so much because they want to come to the United States, but rather in most cases because they simply do not have other alternatives in their country. All of this presents continuing challenges for those of us in the United States who are the logical first responders to newer Salvadorans' needs. Those of us who have been here for some time will contribute as much as we can, making every effort possible to do so. I think that what we did throughout the 1980s has had positive repercussions in terms of our preparedness to play this role now. Of course, we would have liked for our results and impacts to be even better, but we have much to be proud of in terms of what we have left behind for coming generations to build on.

Our challenge now is indeed to build on what has been accomplished over the past decades since we established ourselves in this country. We still have work to do. For example, too many of our people are still not U.S. citizens and cannot vote in this country. That poses an ongoing challenge for us, to take people to become citizens and then to register them to vote; that is the only way to gain a stronger voice in the North American system of governance. If we work now at this problem, I believe that, in ten years, our community will have more recognition and benefits at all levels of U.S. life: politically and economically. All this has to do with our community's desire to succeed, to get more involved, to vote, to get informed; it requires those who have not become citizens to do so in order to participate and influence this country at all levels on behalf of our broader community.

I think that, within ten years, if we consider and nurture all the young Salvadorans who are now studying, we will have more of our people in strategic places and institutional entities. It is imperative for our continuing advancement that the Salvadoran youths who are studying today continue helping the community as they graduate and take on professional and other life responsibilities.

My future is likely to keep me in the struggle for justice. Though I am no longer that young, I still have much to contribute. As to where I might make my next contributions, I sometimes experience conflicting feelings. Once in a while, I see myself staying in Los Angeles, continuing to work with the community here. Other times, I see myself retiring and returning to El Salvador. I have often dreamt of going over there to pass my final years; but most of my family is here, so I do not know how realistic that would be. These days, I find myself thinking in terms of health promotion and the need to advance that work among our people in El Salvador. There is such a relative lack of wellness information available to the people there and I would like to go there, therefore, to lead a health promotion campaign. Only time will tell whether this is what I end up doing in the years to come.

The important note to close on is that we all have something to contribute toward the betterment of humanity and our world. In my own life, I have personally experienced the transformative power of participation. I can testify that even the poorest and most disadvantaged people of our community can be empowered if we continue to become more active in life here in the United States. We all have something to contribute and we must. We are a growing community of immigrants, a fairly new community that already has reached some important achievements. I want our people to become more aware of the fact that we have power. I want to invite them to participate, to seek information and ideas that can help to make our community stronger.

We almost always look around our immediate area and we say, "We're okay," but we generally do not look further than that. If you look at me, for example, my family and I are not bad off, we have possibilities and all that; but if you look beyond, there are so many needs still in our community. More people should get involved in community organizations. There is so much to do, so many ways to contribute to the community. I cannot summarize our collective experience during and since the war, but we can see how each one of us has contributed with at least a grain of sand to having found our way from the worst of possibilities to what is today a much more opportunistic place for our people.

This is merely to say that the sacrifices and hard work of people in a community do finally matter. All the work that we did here in the United States after leaving our country had repercussions in El Salvador in terms of slowing and then finally stopping the persecutions. Many of us were persecuted in the United States, too. We can never forget the letters from the death squads that many of us received. I was a target for them, too. One time they drained the brake fluid in my car and on several occasions they came looking for me at my home. Another time, two men kidnapped and terrorized me. I was going to a meeting and they intercepted me on the street. They took me to Elysian Park and left me there after warning me that their action was merely a first reprimand for my involvement in the movement. Then, some months later, I was with a colleague coming out of a meeting at CARECEN and a passing vehicle shot at my car. The bullet hit the gas tank. We were lucky that the car did not explode. The Los Angeles Police Department still has that information on file, but the LAPD never did investigate the matter.

Many people still today, even many within our own community, do not realize that these things happened throughout the 1980s here in this country. Our adversaries both in the United States and in El Salvador harassed us relentlessly. Even members of the death squads in El Salvador occasionally came to the United States and stalked or persecuted us. But we did not remain quiet, nor did we back down. We made it known to our enemies that we would not be intimidated and we showed them as much through our continuing actions. That ultimately stopped them. Today, it is incredible to recall that these things happened in this country. Who would have thought that possible?

There are important lessons in these reflections. I hope that our younger emerging community leaders will hold these reflections close in their thoughts as they take up greater responsibilities in the future. One of my largest sources of gratification is that my daughter, in her own way, has carried forward the work of social justice and the promotion of peace that she inherited from me. In her work at an organization called Homies Unidos, she encourages young people involved in gangs to pursue constructive paths to education, employment and community service. In this work, she builds on lessons she learned from me and others of my generation that reveal the redeeming values of peace and humanity over violence and greed. I hope her and others of her generation will be able to find ways to greatly expand their efforts in these directions in the years to come. While the challenges still before them are certainly large, I pray that those like my daughter will be able to carry forward what we attempted to put in place on their behalf. In this connection, I hope that we will have provided them with at least some inspiration, direction and confidence that treating society's larger problems and dangers is finally a worthy and honorable calling.

Ramón Cardona

My name is Juan Ramón Cardona and I am from El Salvador. I grew up in San Salvador. My mother and her generation of brothers and sisters were the first to come to the national capitol. They came from the countryside where my grandparents had lived all their lives. I was thus born on the outskirts of the capitol city in a suburban hillside community. I remember very well when I was very young, perhaps three or four years old, one day we took up all of our belongings and all of our relatives—because we were a large family—and we left on a bus to move to a house in the Dina neighborhood, an old marginal area in south San Salvador.

Our move from the suburbs to the capitol was a significant departure. For years, our family had lived in Planes de Renderos, south of San Salvador, on top of a tall set of bluffs that were rural and pastoral. My grandfather had inherited some lands there, but unfortunately he did not manage them correctly. So, little by little he had to sell them off to survive. The last available parcel was sold just so that we could afford to move to San Salvador. This was in the late 1940s. Our house in the Dina neighborhood of San Salvador establishes my earliest memory of home life. In time, I was moved with twenty other members of my family to what was an old inn, one of the few properties we could afford that would accommodate all of us.

I left El Salvador in the late 1960s. My father had already immigrated to the San Francisco Bay Area in the mid-1950s to seek employment. Many other Salvadoran men had done the same after World War II, thus establishing an early incipient Central American enclave in and around San Francisco. After a little more than a decade working in the Bay Area, my father had saved enough money to submit the necessary immigration documents, secure a larger home and purchase bus tickets enabling the rest of our family to join him. That is how we came to live in Oakland in the late 1960s. I was a teenager at the time of my arrival; I was fourteen years old.

At that time, it took between six and seven days to make the journey by bus from San Salvador to Oakland. We traveled almost without stopping, transferring from one bus to the other along the way. I remember that we came through Mexico to El Paso, Texas. We were there for two days and I went out briefly onto the street during our layover. A passing policeman started questioning my brother and me. The only English that we knew was "No English yet;" my father had taught us that, and that is how we answered the policeman's questions. He was asking us why were we not in school since we were obviously of school age. We got that only much later. The policeman then seemed to realize that we were in transit, not locals, and he let us go back to the bus depot to reconnect with our other family members.

In the years that followed, I went to high school in Oakland. After that, I was able to enroll at a local community college. During this period, Chicano community activists had pressed California state authorities to open college and university doors to more Latino students, making the entry requirements more flexible. I benefited directly from this activism. In a couple of years, I graduated from the community college with an associate degree and gained admission to U.C. Berkeley. This was in the mid-1970s.

Shortly after I started studying at Berkeley, a university massacre took place in San Salvador. At the heart of the tragedy was a seemingly innocuous controversy over El Salvador's decision to host the Miss Universe Pageant. The government was committing many millions of dollars to the beauty pageant, seemingly to demonstrate the nation's standing to host a major international event. But, at the same time, many millions of Salvadoran people were suffering from chronic hunger and unemployment. Under the circumstances, the large expenditure of national treasure for a mere beauty pageant seemed highly inappropriate to many Salvadorans. Some workers and university students decided to outwardly protest this folly. When they commenced their demonstration they were brutally fired on and killed by heavily armed police personnel. There had been other massacres in El Salvador in the recent past, in small towns. Indian groups had been slaughtered in well-chronicled genocides dating back to the 1930s.

But the mass killing at the university was unprecedented in our nation. It was especially repressive, brutal and disturbing.

Many not killed in the massacre were detained and treated very severely. Some protestors were detained and never again accounted for. These developments were shocking to Salvadorans here in the United States. I had never before been involved in politics, but I too was very affected by the news of these developments in El Salvador. Throughout my teen years in the United States, my family and I had maintained close contact with our relatives back home. Every year, we would visit and spend considerable time in our country to retain and renew our ties there vís-a-vís close family members and friends. The university massacre was thus something very close to us, not some distant and abstract occurrence. Being a university student myself, I was especially affected by these killings.

In the aftermath of the massacre, Radio KOFY, one of the few Bay Area Spanish radio stations at that time, invited its interested listeners to a meeting where the massacre would be discussed and strategies considered in relation to how we should all respond. I shared this information with some other students I knew on the U.C. campus and four of us went to the KOFY-sponsored discussion. A follow up meeting was organized by the Comité de Salvadoreños Progresistas (the Committee of Progressive Salvadorans), which I believe is the first Salvadoran committee that was established in the United States to offer solidarity to the Salvadoran people as a result of what was happening in our country. Almost immediately, people in Los Angeles, New York and other major U.S. cities also formed solidarity committees.

The Comité de Salvadoreños Progresistas had only been founded a few weeks earlier, and as its first major activity the group organized an assembly in front of the Salvadoran consulate in San Francisco to repudiate the massacre. I was encouraged to participate at the protest gathering. The event established my christening as an activist and it coincided ironically with the day on which I was to leave for El Salvador for a long-planned vacation trip to visit family members. When I arrived later that evening in El Salvador there was a lot of social activity and several large public demonstrations. Many of my cousins, with whom I had been raised, especially the eldest, Pepe, were already involved in these groups. I participated as an observer.

The demonstrations took place in Park La Plaza de La Libertad, in downtown San Salvador. I heard speeches and attended several rallies. I was struck at the time by how young the opposition leaders were; many of them were only my age. I think that sealed my desire to support their cause and to learn more about the issues. Until then, there had just been a vague call for democratic ideals in El Salvador, but the massacre put all the issues in relief for me. I committed myself to start working with the Solidarity Movement that was just then forming, and when I returned from El Salvador I became deeply involved in that work.

Many factors had informed the growing sense of social justice that finally compelled me to become an activist in the Solidarity Movement. Because of my youthful energy and rebelliousness, the nature of the times, the fact that I was a student at U.C. Berkeley—all of these things made me think in terms of utopias. I cannot say that I was an adherent of Marxism, Leninism, communism or subversion as a result. But I felt strongly that the kind of poverty and suffering that afflicted nations like El Salvador simply should not exist. I felt this very intuitively; I also lived it through personal experiences and observations going back to my early youth.

In the years after my father came to the United States and stayed here for many years without us, sending us only sporadic help, my mother had to work very hard to support our family. She was a hair stylist. She had to go from town to town looking for work. I was responsible for distributing flyers that we produced to advertise her services, explaining where she was and the many fashionable haircuts she could produce. We often struggled financially. As a consequence, our family sometimes did not have enough food to sustain us. Sometimes, all that we had to get by on were tortillas and sour cream and perhaps a little bit of salt. We had no money to buy more than the most basic clothing available and then only in single quantities. When we had to repair the single pair of shoes we each owned, we would take them to the shoe repairman and he would take two days to fix them. During those two days, we would not go to school because we were too embarrassed to go barefoot.

As I grew older and looked back on these experiences, I would think that it was plainly unjust for people to have to live this way, while others benefited from luxuries and privileges that were exceptional and exclusive. That is how my response to the university massacre evolved from initial shock and disbelief to outrage. I found myself feeling in an increasingly profound way that it was simply unacceptable for the government to have taken such an extreme measure to quell what were finally not unreasonable concerns about its choices.

In subsequent years, I sought to be part of an organized response. In the Bay Area, through the Comité de Salvadoreños Progresistas, we published a newspaper called *El Pulgarcito Rojo* (The Little Red Thumb). It was edited by Carlos Vela, an associate who later became influential in the development of the Solidarity Movement and related aid activities. I went to study in Mexico as part of a student-exchange program between U.C. Berkeley and the National Autonomous University of Mexico (UNAM) in Mexico City. Upon my return, with other movement supporters, we started the Comité Centroamericano de Trabajadores y Estudiantes (the Central American Workers and Students Committee).

By this time, large social movements in El Salvador, like the Bloque Popular Revolucionario (the Popular Revolutionary Block), or BPR, and later LP28, were getting underway to challenge the government's increasingly repressive policies. These indigenous opposition efforts influenced diversely situated movement sympathizers in the United States and elsewhere and we were contacted by BPR for assistance. A group of us organized ourselves, accordingly, to help. We worked a lot with the experiences and lessons of solidarity that Nicaragua and Chile had left us. A lot of this led us to connect with progressive leaders within the Catholic Church.

Father Moriarti was a particularly important early supporter of our work in the Bay Area. He not only lent us his church for planning meetings and public gatherings, but he also offered us his back office equipment like telephones, copiers and printers. In addition, he helped us intellectually by pushing us at every step of the way to clarify what we were doing and why. He helped us to pursue our work with greater logic and supporting strategic clarity. He was very influential in our evolving efforts. Along the way, he helped us to better understand and respect the role of the church in the struggle for social justice and how it also sought to advance human and civil rights. Father Moriarti accompanied us from the beginning in the campaigns we organized to demand the liberation of political prisoners in El Salvador. Shortly thereafter, several North American leaders, Anglos primarily, started to participate with us in solidarity.

We were skeptical from the outset about partnering with such far left groups as Trotskyites, Communists and Maoists. These factions wanted to get close to us, but we regarded them with distrust because they came with a terminology, a Marxist-Leninist lingo that we did not understand at that time. We also worried about their agendas. We received early warnings about these groups from established friends of our growing movement. "Be careful with those groups because the only thing that they want is to control the movement," many told us. As a result of these concerns, we tended to look to partners who we considered to be independent, rather than doctrinaire, and we formed strong alliances with them. We did not partner with any networks or organizations that we felt were not genuinely committed to advancing our cause the way we defined its terms.

The early collaboration with the Catholic Church through Father Moriarti ultimately led to allied partnerships with thirty-two different religious denominations that in time became involved in the Sanctuary Movement: an effort to protect at-risk Central American refugees from repatriation to their nations of origin for fear of their consequent killing, torture or persecution. The additional religious leaders that comprised our increasingly powerful sanctuary network were Jewish, Protestant, Baptist and Lutheran. The rich diversity of the religious leaders and denominations that came to our support gave us powerful leverage with important stakeholders including movement donors, the media and powerful U.S. and international political figures. Their involvement with us in advancing our demand that human rights in El Salvador be respected was especially helpful.

Our North American partners taught us many new basic political and organizing skills that we used effectively in our evolving campaign. They exposed us to the power of house parties, raffles and bazaars. They introduced our cause to new technologies and strategic lobbying tactics. They also helped us to vet our core concepts and objectives as we progressed in our work. We quickly adapted the new tools and learnings made available through our friends to the growing needs of our movement.

An important manifestation of our resulting political prowess emerged in 1979 when a group of friends and I started Los Amigos Estaodunidenses de la Revolución Salvadoreña (The U.S. Friends of the Salvadoran Revolution). This new organization provided a formal framework around which we could more advantageously activate the cross-denominational leadership we had assembled in the form of various religious principals. It also enabled us to better mobilize around our strategies related to defending human rights in Salvador, establishing a youth group, and raising public funds. This, added on to our solidarity work, culminated all of our hard work and achievements to that point.

Young leaders like me who were involved in this work were growing leaps and bounds as a result of our exposure to it. I continued taking classes during this period at U.C. Berkeley in Latin American Studies. But the experience that I had gained through my Solidarity Movement activities was quickly beginning to outpace my school-based learning. This experience now took me in entirely unanticipated directions—directions, it turned out, which prepared me much more for public and academic leadership than I would have ever guessed possible.

After having come to the U.C. Berkeley campus as a very immature, timid immigrant, I now spoke regularly and confidently at well-attended public meetings. I also found myself playing an increasingly visible role as the leader of important new campus initiatives with a political inclination. With fellow students, for example, I helped to start a new campus organization around this time called ADELA, La Asociación de Estudiantes Latinoamericanos (the Latin American Students Association).

In 1980 there occurred a terrible event that dramatically affected me and our movement. I was working at a nonprofit institution known as Clínica de la Raza in Oakland, a community health clinic where I was responsible for prevention programs. As part of my responsibilities in this work, I would go to schools and talk with students about drugs, sex education and other social issues in a group atmosphere. On one occasion when I was preparing to conduct a site visit, I heard the first news of a group of Salvadorans abandoned by a *coyote* that was bringing them illegally into the United States through Arizona. It turned out that thirteen members of the party of twenty-six Salvadoran refugees had died in the punishing desert heat. The remaining refugees had survived in varying degrees of health.

Local activists immediately held an emergency meeting. We wanted to carefully decide how to respond to the case unfolding in Arizona, because we knew that if any of the surviving Salvadorans were deported they would almost surely later be found dead, as the military in El Salvador considered anyone who tried to flee the country to be subversive. So Adam Kiufel, a friend of mine, and I were sent by our Bay Area colleagues to Ajo, Arizona, near Tucson, to assess the situation and to ensure that the survivors would not be turned over to the Salvadoran authorities.

My firsthand experience seeing all the people who died in this tragedy and listening to the recounts of survivors was horrifying. The survivors spoke about their desperation and the sheer craziness they experienced being abandoned in an enclosed trailer in more than 100-degree heat. They were more than fortunate to have lived through the ordeal. Those who were not so lucky became martyrs whose sacrifice fueled even greater commitment to the resistance movements we and others were beginning to organize. The plight of the thirteen Salvadoran refugees who died in the Arizona desert galvanized new national attention to the crisis in El Salvador and also spurred the Sanctuary Movement to new heights of community and public support.

My experience in the Arizona desert also redoubled my own dedication to solidarity and sanctuary work. Upon my return to California, therefore, I threw myself into the movement completely. I also spent more time at La Clínica de la Raza. A few months later I was asked to be a spokesperson for the Frente Democrático Revolucionario (the Revolutionary Democratic Front, or FDR). The FDR was playing a central role in advancing unity efforts that were beginning to take shape among opposition groups in El Salvador. Those discussions had at their core the notion of all the opposition groups galvanizing behind support for new social investments and a reformed politico-military order in El Salvador.

Various unions, university and high school student groups, and political parties in opposition to the sitting government formed the core of the FDR. Together, they began to develop a proposed reform agenda that included a petition to U.S. governmental leaders to cease American support for the Salvadoran government and military. To advance this important work, I and various allied organizational colleagues across the U.S. began traveling to different North American cities to denounce the human rights abuses and violations that the Salvadoran government was supporting at that time. We also called for the U.S. government not to intervene with additional military support in El Salvador, which was resulting counterproductively in the purchase of arms and the training of paramilitary personnel—all of which was merely serving to further repress the Salvadoran people.

The U.S. government's stated goal at this point was to dramatically augment the size of the Salvadoran army, which had until then been about 10,000-12,000 soldiers. Officials in the Reagan administration wanted to enlarge the size of that force tenfold. They particularly wanted to bolster specialized units with sophisticated weaponry to quell rebel forces that were increasingly challenging government positions. As the United States push to escalate the conflict in El Salvador proceeded, so too did our resistance efforts.

A large part of our response targeted public and political opinion leaders in the United States. In this connection, I began to play an ever-growing role during this period as a professional opposition spokesperson. Thereafter, I served as a representative of important international advocacy organizations and various local and state governments sympathetic to our calls for a change in course in El Salvador and more humane immigration policies and responses where U.S.-based Salvadorans were concerned. For the most part we concentrated this work in Washington, DC, where we targeted both members of the congress and the senate to join our cause.

I was also frequently invited during this time to travel to other English-speaking countries, including some of the Caribbean island nations, to broaden support for an anti-Salvadoran government resolution at the United Nations. Each year, the U.N. general assembly was advancing strong debate on our issues, most of it favorable to our position. To consolidate our position, I consulted with leading diplomats from about fifteen different governments. I also visited Surinam, Guyana and Belize to obtain official support from those nations. In addition, I traveled to Canada several times to advance our diplomatic support base and to encourage Salvadoran communities that had organized there to continue with the solidarity struggle that was taking place in support of the Salvadoran revolutionary movement.

In different ways, my efforts were intended to encourage and promote solidarity through broad-based regional leadership education. Supporting this work is what I did for close to two years, explaining to regional and foreign leaders the reasons why the civil war was taking place in El Salvador, the nature and aims of the revolutionary movement and so on. At each turn I denounced the U.S. interventionism of the time because of its biased position of only providing support to the Salvadoran establishment while attempting to create an entire strategy against rebel factions seeking national reforms. In many documented cases, the common people were the greatest victims of the Salvadoran government's initiatives and military attacks.

Subsequently, here in the United States, I traveled through almost the entire country. I went to about forty different states. It was incredible to witness the help, solidarity and sympathy that we received from different religious groups, universities, students, professors and Salvadoran community members. Each group was different, but they were all committed to human rights and democracy in the Americas. All of them responded to our various calls to action. I would talk to their representatives and followers at various university forums; it was not unusual to have 200-300 people in the audience at each of these gatherings. The North American solidarity groups that were already established benefited substantially from the great sympathy that our campaigns, mobilizations and other activities generated. We promoted a lot of delegations that traveled directly to El Salvador to support the refugee repatriation movement and to protect those who were living under serious threats of Salvadoran governmental abuse or assassination.

The profile and presence of Salvadoran community leaders was considerable at the many events we organized across the United States. Typically, we would speak at universities, churches and public forums. Interviews with media were plentiful, and we also held many well-attended press conferences. We took good advantage of the opportunity to publicize our objectives and to explain the political and military situation that was keeping the Salvadoran people oppressed. We also educated and informed many audiences about the history behind the unrest in Central America. Through our efforts we reached many thousands of people of goodwill who became supporters of our cause.

This work was exciting and important, yet grueling. We were on the road constantly. Between my travels from California to the Caribbean and then to Washington D.C., Canada and various European cities, if I was home for 30 days without having to travel, that was a lot in those days. It was incredible how much we moved around. This is because there was a high demand for us to travel from here to there, to represent the oppositional and revolutionary forces at that time. The events coming out of El Salvador during this period were shocking. The assassination of Monsignor Oscar A. Romero and a group of North American nuns, the internationally known Sumpul and Mozote massacres, the murder of various FDR leaders, of entire committees of union leaders who were assassinated collectively—all of these atrocities underscored the depth of our opposition's lack of respect for humanity and the rule of law. The very nature of these abhorrent developments helped many people to become aware of the need to change the regime in El Salvador.

In one instance, as I made my way around to increase public awareness of our work, I personally found myself at risk of being lost to the madness of the times. I was coming back from Puerto Rico, from a university conference on Latin American social movements. I had traveled from San Juan to Miami to Honduras, and from there I was going on to Nicaragua. In Tegucigalpa, at the airport, I was kidnapped and taken to an underground jail. I had been carrying a newspaper from the Puerto Rican Socialist Party, called *Claridad* (Clarity), where my photo was featured along with an interview. I had also collected, and was therefore carrying, some progressive literature from the Caribbean, given that I had been assigned to that area recently. Merely having this material appeared to be the basis for my apprehension.

From the Tegucigalpa jail, I was taken to another one. My kidnappers beat me, interrogated me and tortured me. At a certain point, I began to worry that I would be killed in their custody. But I was ultimately saved. Because there were strong solidarity campaigns both in

Puerto Rico and in the United States, and because the leaders of those movements knew that I was missing in Nicaragua, the Nicaraguan and Salvadoran governments were ultimately forced to acknowledge that I had been incarcerated. Later, they offered the explanation that I had used fraudulent documents to travel as the basis of my jailing. But that was an outright fabrication of the facts. I always traveled with my U.S. permanent residency card and I had that documentation on me when I was apprehended in Tegucigalpa.

My release was sealed when a delegation of key U.S. leaders and friends showed up in Nicaragua to demand justice on my behalf. The delegation included, among others, Bay Area Congressman Ronald Dellums, a representative of San Francisco's Archbishop Quinn and a lawyer from the American Union for Human Rights. Upon arrival, they pressed both the U.S. embassy in Managua and responsible Nicaraguan officials to assist in securing my release. They also successfully encouraged the Honduran government to favorably intercede. Their direct intervention on my behalf probably saved my life. It was already well-documented by this time that almost 200 Salvadorans who were captured in Honduras and accused of being subversive had been disappeared in recent years. I was fortunate to have had those people exert sufficient pressure on my behalf, that I was ultimately freed. It did not have to work out that way, necessarily.

Once back in the United States, I became more involved again in institution building efforts that our movement and our people needed to prevail, both in relation to the war in El Salvador and the quest for a successful integration into U.S. life. This involved a good deal of collective work. Many good people were involved. It was around this time that we decided the various refugee committees and supporting circles of North American friends and human rights groups were not enough. We needed to develop still additional vehicles to fuel the longer term viability of Salvadorans in the United States.

Many of us thus turned our attention to the creation of new national support networks and organizations such as Medical Aid for El Salvador. Medical Aid for El Salvador mainly involved artists and Hollywood actors who came together to support the creation of new financial institutions for the long term benefit of Salvadoran community members. Some of this work continues to the present, with a focus on economic sustainability projects and the promotion of supporting social, cultural, athletic and scientific projects. We also redoubled our efforts to advance the work of key community support organizations like CARECEN, Centro de Recursos Centroamericanos (the Central American Resource Center), which helped to lead our charge to secure a temporary protected status for Salvadoran and other Central American refugees, so that our people could remain in the United States while the worst of the war and risks to their safety in El Salvador raged on. Finally, we facilitated the development of various documentary and public educational projects including books and films, to help establish a stronger platform on which to galvanize U.S. public and institutional support for our work.

We carried this work forward throughout the 1980s, but it was not until the early 1990s, with the culmination of the peace treaties of that era, that the nightmare in El Salvador finally came to an end. With these developments, many of us had the opportunity to become involved in efforts to ensure transparent, free and democratic elections in the country, as well as the promotion of new human rights and political protections in El Salvador. We had to be absolutely certain that we could see fundamental reforms in the nation's governance that would preclude forevermore the well-founded fear of many surviving Salvadorans that death squads and assassins might still come at night and kidnap and/or kill them, as had happened to many people over the prior years.

The movement to transform El Salvador into a truly democratic state is now almost twenty years old. The leaders and supporters of organizations like those I was involved in made a huge contribution to the Salvadoran cause by organizing and standing in solidarity with our brothers and sisters in El Salvador during the worst of the violence, as well as in its aftermath. We coalesced with one another as Salvadoran expatriates and we augmented our own voices by recruiting countless North American religious leaders, human rights activists, politicians, university executives and students to our cause. It was a huge undertaking, but ultimately a worthy and successful one.

Since the conclusion of the peace treaties I have been sporadically involved in various aspects of Salvadoran community and electoral politics. During the 1994 elections in El Salvador, for example, I became involved in supporting presidential candidate Rubén Zamora and his vice presidential candidate, Mr. Lima of the FMLN party, El Salvador's progressive wing. I accompanied Zamora when he traveled through the United States and assisted his fundraising efforts. But, in the main, I increasingly re-focused my life around more intellectual and U.S.-based institution building pursuits with the end of the El Salvador war. I returned to U.C. Berkeley and I completed my undergraduate degree. I also started a new initiative that has provided transnational social and economic support to the former conflict zones in El Salvador, the Instituto para el Desarrollo de la Nueva Democrácia, USA-El Salvador (the Institute for the Development of New Democracy, USA-El Salvador). In addition, in 1995, I founded the Centro Latino Cuscatlán, in large part to focus on ways to regulate the migratory status of the hundreds of thousands of Salvadorans and Central Americans seeking permanent residency in the United States each year and to facilitate Salvadoran citizenship promotion and voting in the United States.

By 1996, though, I had become executive director of CARECEN in San Francisco. CARECEN has become over the years the Central American community's most powerful and influential support and advocacy network. There are five CARECEN offices in the United States. The first one was established in Washington, DC in May 1981. Allied CARECEN offices were subsequently developed in the mid-1980s in New York, Los Angeles and Houston. The last office, the one I took over in the mid-1990s, was opened in San Francisco in May 1987.

After becoming executive director of CARECEN's San Francisco office, I merged the work of Centro Latino Cuscatlán into that of CARECEN. I stayed at the helm of CARECEN for seven years. During this time, I almost tripled the institution's budget to $1.3 million in 2004. I also expanded programs in areas ranging from social assistance to health services to family assistance. I also further strengthened our work related to immigration advocacy. We accomplished a great deal during my tenure as CARECEN's executive director and I am proud of that. We faced some setbacks in California as a result of growing anti-immigrant sentiment across the state and the country;

but overall we helped our community to further advance during this period.

When I think about the future, I see it positively. I believe Salvadorans fare favorably when compared to other nationalities that have came to the United States, as far as progress achieved in the first, second and third generations following arrival. Quite a number of first generation Salvadorans have done well since coming to this nation. Our people have overcome considerable hardships and yet found a way nevertheless to resettle in this nation, to become productive contributors to the economy and to form dynamic and innovative associations. Our accomplishments on an organizational level have been very sophisticated and advanced.

Today, each year, Salvadorans in this country support several billion dollars in social and economic investments in El Salvador through private remittances—bank wire transfers that help family members and communities in our country of origin. Through this work, we have helped development committees especially in smaller towns across El Salvador—subdivisions and neighborhoods that otherwise have limited access to capital—to support important infrastructure projects or youth programs. Recently, U.S.-based committees in Los Angeles, San Francisco and Virginia, for example, have raised many thousands of dollars to build a new sports center in Santa Elena Usulután. That kind of work continues to be very important; we should applaud those who have made it possible. They deserve our praise.

Looking ahead, I think we still need to establish a more integrated politics between El Salvador and here. El Salvador's government has been working hard in recent years to move the nation forward, but it has not yet established a well-coordinated program with the U.S.-based Salvadoran community. We would all benefit from closer relations and coordination. I think that from El Salvador we can strengthen the bonds with those who are here, especially those involved with the various development committees and home country associations, to educate them about ways to work more strategically in El Salvador to better address issues of chronic unemployment and extreme poverty there.

For our part, those of us Salvadorans who reside here now could do a better job of working with Salvadoran authorities to streamline the integration process for the more then 400 Salvadorans who migrate to the United States still each day. Such coordination would provide Salvadoran newcomers with a greater sense of reference with respect to our organizations here in terms of available assistance when they look for employment, housing, family support, educational assistance, health services and English language training support. There is so much more we can still do together to align the interests and benefits available to Salvadorans who are here as well as those who remain there.

In the United States, our challenges ahead mainly have to do with issues of youth development, cultural preservation and related concerns. Our children are being raised here, they are growing up here, and many have been born here. The level of influence that we have on them is limited in regards to how they identify with their roots, with where we come from. Various community institutions, networks and programs can help to fortify the bonds between our older and younger generations, through projects and programs here in the United States that advance learning about our history, such as documentaries, books like this one and educational interventions through which public school teachers can be trained and encouraged to teach the Salvadoran national anthem, as well as arts and cultural traditions of El Salvador.

As for me, my future will almost certainly continue to involve me in community-focused activism. Last year, I reopened the Centro Latino Cuscatlán. We are working with Salvadorans and Latinos in the Bay Area who face continuing immigration challenges, to advance proposals to achieve needed immigration reforms. We each have to contribute at least a grain of salt as we move through life. I have tried to do this for many years now. I feel that I still have more to give. For example, I want to strengthen the bonds between our U.S.-based Salvadoran groups and the various non-governmental organizations (NGOs) in El Salvador that share our interests and concerns. Together, I am persuaded there is much more we can do to advance the sort of projects I have spoken about earlier here—projects for youth, culture, sports, tourism, etc. I think that over the next five years, it is very likely that I will become more involved in this kind of work.

Overall, I expect many good things to emerge from El Salvador and the Salvadoran people in the next phase of our journey. I recently came back from El Salvador; after several years of absence, and I was deeply affected by the will to struggle that has remained strong in the communities, individuals and organizations working to transform the country. I also learned of groups there that are trying to document what has happened in the last thirty years of El Salvador's history, the antecedents of the war, the civil war and the aftermath of the peace treaties. Capturing this collective history and its lessons is extremely timely and important work. This book, which assembles the testimonies of individuals who had a key role in developing the Solidarity Movement in the United States, is also an extremely valuable contribution to our transnational community's evolution. Here in the United States there is a lot of history related to our struggle that needs still to be recorded. Without these recounts we heighten our risk of forgetting, of repeating history's worst chapters.

The need to remain vigilant, while also celebrating our past victories is a constant. We have overcome many daunting obstacles to find ourselves today in a position of great promise and potential as a people. But there are no guarantees to continued future success and forward movement. Conditions all around our hemisphere should give us reason for pause. Circumstances in El Salvador today, though far better than twenty or more years ago, are nevertheless a cause for concern. My most recent trip to El Salvador—my first in about five years—underscored this. I was dismayed to learn how the long term affects of chronic poverty are driving many Salvadorans to despair. Wherever I went during my most recent travels in El Salvador, I saw relatives and friends. In each place, I was pressed with requests for assistance. "Ramón, why don't you help me to go to the United States?" "Ramón, is there anything your organization can do to help us with more funding?"

In the long run, this lingering want for opportunity and resources is very harmful to the country and to international stability. El Salvador's youthful labor force is leaving, along with many professionals, in increasingly growing numbers. The nation is thus experiencing a significant brain drain. While El Salvador has certainly stabilized in recent years, its future as a continuing peaceful democracy is hardly certain. We need to redouble our efforts therefore to ensure its success in the years to come.

Finally, I think we need to leave a more visceral record of the El Salvador war experience that our future generations will always be able to look to. I think that this was a chapter in the history of our nation that warrants continual revisitation. We should never forget it. So in addition to producing more books and studies on this history and publicly circulating supporting documents, photographs and the like, in future years, we also need to mount major new monuments to the thousands and thousands of Salvadorans who died or otherwise sacrificed during the war of the 1980s. These were the great heroes whose experiences should serve as enduring reminders of the responsibilities we must continue to honor if the Salvadoran people are to survive and thrive in the years ahead.

Eduardo A. González, M.D.

My name is Eduardo Antonio González Martínez. I am from San Salvador, El Salvador. For a long time, when I worked in the Solidarity Movement and with allied aid projects, I assumed an alias to protect myself from possible retaliation by government agents and their reactionary supporters. During this period, many people knew me as Guillermo Rodezno. Today, some who knew me by this assumed identity still have a hard time getting used to my real name.

During my formative years, many events left an impression on me that bear on my ultimate experiences in Solidarity. It is hard to say which of these was the most important, but certainly one key factor that marked my early journey profoundly is that I grew up in a family headed by a single mother. Although my father was part of my life, for all practical purposes my mother was both father and mother. In our family, I was the only man. I was raised by my mother, my grandmother, a few aunts and some female cousins, all women. I think this marked me in more than one sense. Perhaps the most significant is that I have always been very sensitive to the needs of women and of their way of thinking, which has been a great asset because I have never had a difficult time adapting to the presence of women, whether in work or in other situations.

Another factor or life experience that marked me a lot early on was that my family was very religious. Since I was a child, I have been called to embrace the importance of not only thinking about myself, but also, and even more profoundly, the needs of others around me. In this sense, I grew up with a spiritual, religious, and social sensitivity. In addition, I came from a lower middle-class family that suffered hardships. We struggled at times. And yet we were not poor. In fact, we had some comparative privileges that created in us a sense of social responsibility. In spite of the needs with which we lived, we could clearly see in our community and nation that there were many people in even more difficult situations than we faced. As a result, I remember that my family was always trying to help those less fortunate; we made ourselves available to do something for others in need. I think that influenced me a quite a bit.

Another thing that was also very important is that I grew up in a family where stories of important historical and political passages were told and valued. My grandmother especially liked to tell these stories. I would listen attentively to her and by doing so I learned a lot about the history of El Salvador—things I would never really learn about at school. She would recount stories and memories from the era of early-to-mid twentieth century Salvadoran presidents: Martínez, for example, who became president of the republic during her young adulthood and his predecessor Dr. Molina, both of whom she actually met. She would speak of what life was like in El Salvador at that time. She would talk about things like the government-supported massacre of Indians that took place in 1932, which resulted in the deaths of people she knew personally.

I did not know at the time how much of my grandmother's storytelling was fiction, imagination or hearsay. But her stories made me very curious about the history of El Salvador. When I later read books about El Salvador's modern history as an adult, many of the events that my grandmother had told me about were chronicled. There were even some names referenced in these readings that she had mentioned during my childhood. For me, this was really important because, in an oral form, perhaps in the most traditional form of how history has been transmitted across the generations, my grandmother encouraged me to take an interest in our history and in how El Salvador had suffered, especially the population that lived through tyrannies, massacres and under the military governments of the 1930s.

The insights transmitted to me through my grandmother's stories left an important mark on me. Over the years, they gave context to many of the experiences that ultimately led me and so many others to leave El Salvador during the 1980s. Ironically, I ultimately left El Salvador under circumstances comparable to those that marked my grandmother's early life experiences. In the scheme of this reality, however, my story was quite simple and not nearly as dramatic or sad as the stories of many of my compatriots. In fact, my story and experience, at least to the point of my exodus from El Salvador, might be described as somewhat average. Each step in the process that led to my leaving my country added an additional layer

In 1970 I started studying in a Catholic school for boys. It was quite a shock for me to move from a home filled with women to an all-boys school where all the teachers, priests, were men. That is where I had my first social trauma; everything was different and difficult to adjust to. The school was very strict. Although my mother could at times be very stern, the school environment presented a much more challenging kind of strictness and discipline. For the first time in my life, a man could physically punish me, for example. In El Salvador, it was still common in those days for teachers to use corporal punishment, and they frequently did. I will never forget this: our teacher had several kinds of bamboo sticks. To discipline us, he would hit us on the front in the groin and then in the back on the buttocks several times. It was very painful. Also, on occasion he would require us to cluster our fingers and he would slam on our fingertips the wooden part of the blackboard eraser.

Such punishments were frequent in my early and middle school years, a common and accepted practice back then. In effect, they were small tortures. These early experiences exposed me for the first time to the power of group psychology. We never questioned any of it. Perhaps what is most important in all this was that it compelled me somehow to get more involved in religious education. At that time, liberation theology was at its peak in Latin America with the Second Vatican Council's recasting of core church protocol and practice. I studied under Salesians, who are very conservative, at least in terms of the intellectual and spiritual development of their students. Compared to their Jesuit counterparts, they were not as involved in social movements or issues. But in the ensuing years in El Salvador, it became almost impossible to separate religious teaching and considerations from the nation's growing social, economic and political problems.

In my subsequent years at Don Bosco during the 1970s, I started to participate in catechism classes that were offered on Sundays. There were buses and train stations in that area, all very close to the police and military headquarters. There were also a number of marginal neighborhoods in the vicinity. The school organized frequent sport activities, which they offered to attract young people from these surrounding neighborhoods and, before or after those activities, they would require participating community members to attend catechism classes. In these encounters, they would prepare children for baptisms, first holy communions and confirmations. I quickly became involved in these activities and as a result I started to discover facts of Salvadoran life that I had never seen or considered.

Because of my family's lower middle-class status and the fact that I had attended a private Catholic school—something that gave me a certain status, aspirations, etc.—I knew early on that I was somewhat privileged. But in the inner city of San Salvador I came to understand for the first time that El Salvador's poverty was much more widespread and problematic than I had ever known. To that point, I had been fairly spared the harsh reality that a majority of Salvadorans faced extreme poverty, hardship and lack of opportunities. This opened my eyes and redoubled my commitment to use religion as a vehicle to help those in need. So with other classmates, I started going to the marginal areas near the school to meet the people who lived there and to invite them to the school church.

Through this work, I met and learned from the people; I saw how they lived in what we know as *champas* (chanti towns). Aside from what I would hear from people—their stories, their dreams—I learned that they faced all kinds of very basic unmet needs. For me it was profoundly eye-opening. I started to ask myself: How could so much poverty exist in our country? As a result, we started a group in this community; it was like a Christian community, a community inside a community, a grassroots theological study group. Inside the Catholic Church we started to discuss and talk of gospel matters and what they meant in the context of the daily lives of the people. For me this was an important engagement that deepened my sense of connection between church teachings and the imperatives of real life public problem-solving.

Around that time, things took an unhappy turn in El Salvador. Latent economic, class and ideological conflicts began to inspire more and more evident social unrest. The government became heavy handed. Right-wing vigilante groups began to terrorize concerned, innocent and poor people suspected of being subversives. These developments took me unexpectedly back to experiences a few years earlier during my elementary and high school years, when the emergence of the conflicts that eventually led to the Central American wars of the 1980s first became visible.

During this earlier time, we had started a theatre group and staged a play called *Luz Negra* (The Dark Light) by Álvaro Menén Desleal, a respected Salvadoran author. The play was strange because the main characters were the heads of two decapitated men. We chose to modify the original text in important ways, adapting it to reflect what was beginning to happen in contemporary El Salvador and much of the rest of Latin America. It was a protest play. Our teacher, who had graduated from La Escuela de Bellas Artes (The School of Fine Arts) in El Salvador, was the director. Other members of the group included Julio, Jaime, Fredie and Margarita.

For many of us, though we did not know it at the time, the school drama project established a very important moment in the development of the artistic and political activism that later would raise awareness in and about El Salvador when widespread violence erupted in the ensuing years. The play offered an important way to raise public awareness of important social and political issues then beginning to affect our country; we presented it in several places and we gained a wide following.

We staged our first performance at the Universidad Nacional (National University). The play's author came to the opening and participated in a post-performance discussion with cast and audience members. In the end, someone asked him what he thought of the modifications we made to his original work and the playwright reported that he thought they were excellent. It was a beautiful experience. Little did we know how relatively short-lived our great success would be. Within a few short years our nation was mired in conflict and mass death. Tragically, I later learned that the teacher who inspired our adaptation and group Director of *Luz Negra* was killed during the war.

In the years that followed my deepening engagement in discussions about religious and theological teachings and social action, I enrolled at the Universidad Nacional. There, I continued my involvement in the grassroots communities I had come to know through my work at the Don Bosco School. In my university studies, I pursued a long-standing but to that point unrealized interest—medicine. I had undertaken my early studies with the idea of becoming a physician. Consistent with my early life learnings and experiences, one of the factors that motivated me in this direction was the desire to help others. During this stage of my journey, the need to help others was beginning to grow dramatically in El Salvador. The war was intensifying and becoming a much more visceral aspect of our daily lives.

Around this time, some friends invited me and several classmates to start visiting Clínica de AGEUS, Asociación General de Estudiantes Universitarios Salvadoreños, (General Association of Salvadoran University Students), which was a student-run health center in those days. The Clínica focused on providing health services to university students. Some of the AGEUS workers and volunteers also helped people outside of the clinic, especially those who had been hurt by the growing conflict, people who had been displaced, shot, physically tortured and abused, etc. As part of our involvement doing this work, AGEUS began educational programs to enable us as health workers to better understand the societal context underlying the increasingly severe injuries we were treating. Our educational efforts provided analysis of the situation in El Salvador, of what was happening on a broader political level. In our course discussions, we started to consider ways that we could raise greater nationwide awareness of what was happening.

It was a time of great excitement among young people especially because there were many events of a political nature taking shape that compelled us to organize and act, even though it was becoming increasingly dangerous to do so. Students and other progressive groups organized dramatic actions and church takeovers. Others took more severe protest measures, burning buses and seizing public offices and embassies, for example. This period was very active with public demonstrations and protests. The Universidad Nacional was under constant attack by the military and paramilitary forces. It was a time of great convulsions. Many of my generation sensed the calling to make history, to make changes, to contribute to better things in El Salvador. We were not driven by a specific, deep political analysis necessarily; rather, we were proceeding from the real life perspective of people under siege. We merely wanted to stop the violence and create a new El Salvador that would offer the people concrete improvements in their quality of life. We felt an urgent calling to do something practical.

All of these developments led me to focus more and more of my energy away from school and onto the struggle for justice. This was not a natural transition for me at the outset. I had always been a person with a lot of clarity about the core significance of education in my life and my studies were consequently a central priority for me. I never fundamentally neglected my studies, but I started to find out more about the popular organizations behind the emerging social movement for change in El Salvador, and I started to become more interested in politics. I never really organized political actions, but I knew people who were involved in this work and I began to collaborate with them. Such involvements took me unwittingly to increasingly dangerous places during this period of my life.

I remember one instance, probably one of the biggest adventures in my life, during the time when I was working at the Clínica de AGEUS, when someone brought several young men to the clinic who had been shot by vigilante supporters of the government. We could not do much for them given our limited surgical facilities at the clinic. We tried to stabilize and resuscitate the wounded rebel youths by inserting into their veins IVs with saline solution. But in order to provide them with the level of care their injuries required, we had to transfer them to a hospital so that they could be treated properly. The greatest problem was figuring out a way do so.

It was not as easy as taking the wounded youth over to a local hospital and telling the admitting staff there, "Here are some people who have been shot, please take them." In the first place, we had inappropriate transportation to safely caravan the patients to a more equipped care facility. Also, we knew that even before getting to the point of gaining their admission to another facility, we would have to pass through security checkpoints along the way that would require us to explain who our patients were, what had happened to them, etc. Our first order challenges were thus logistical: How were we going to get our patients to a hospital to begin with and, once on our way, how were we going to explain to security personnel and others what we were up to without it compromising our patients' or our own security?

We managed to get a pick up truck from the university that we could transform into an ambulance, but we could not find anyone legally qualified to drive it. I could legally drive a passenger car, but I did not have a proper driver's license for the university pick up truck. I volunteered to be the make-shift ambulance driver anyway. Two of the most severely wounded youth in our care were thus carefully placed in the back of the university pick up truck, and a female classmate joined me up front for the trip into town. The clinic management staff on duty carefully instructed my female colleague on how to deal with the situation, what she had to say if we were stopped or apprehended. I knew intuitively that being the driver on this mission would probably be enough to get me at least detained and seriously beaten by the authorities if we were intercepted and things did not go our way.

We decided to transport our wounded patients to the Santa Tecla Hospital named San Juan de Dios, which is close to the Guadalupe Basilica. Sure enough, along the way, we came to a police checkpoint and they stopped us. Honestly, I was terrified and silent. It was the first time I had ever been stopped by police security forces; I had not experienced that before. My female classmate saved us by starting to cry and inventing a compelling explanation for our request to approach the hospital. She said that we were transporting her brother and cousin who had been hurt in an accident. She begged the security checkpoint personnel to let us get the wounded youth to the hospital as soon as possible. To our great relief, the security police let us through without further questions or hassles. We got to the hospital and the girl got out immediately to explain to the medical personnel there why we had come. We deposited the wounded young rebels there and left, having carefully followed the instructions given to us by our clinic managers.

This passage established the first time in my life that I experienced true fear—fear of power and authority—for something that I was doing that was not in fact bad. I was merely tending to people who had suffered severe injuries. But, even I knew by that time in El Salvador that one could be condemned for acts as simple as that; and, so, it created tension and real life danger for me and my classmates who were involved. Ironically, the situation would intensify in future months, though I did not anticipate that at the time. This was still very early in my university medicine program studies.

A little later on, in 1980, one of my friends invited me and several classmates to attend San José de la Montaña seminar, where various refugee groups had assembled to seek safe haven. Many there needed substantial healthcare assistance. I wanted to get my hands busy, to really start practicing medicine, and I also wanted to help those who had assembled in the refugee camp. So I went to San José de la Montaña with a few of my friends and, there, we encountered for the first time the worst atrocities of the war, the terrible injustices carried out against the poor; most of the people there were *campesinos* (peasants). Women, children, elderly people and badly wounded and abused men were heavily represented. Most of them were illiterate, but they would verbally tell us their stories.

Contrary to what we had all hoped for, neither I nor any of my first year medical school classmates was entrusted with any significant responsibilities at the refugee camp. Rather, we were charged to do very basic things, like help prepare food in the camp kitchen. On occasion, we would provide first aid assistance to newer arrivals who had been burned or subjected to more minor injuries. Even less frequently, we would be asked to provide support to medics working with more severely injured refugees. In these instances, we assisted more advanced medical school students engaged with recovering war and torture victims. We would help them; they would tell us what to do.

The experience at the refugee camp further opened my eyes. It gave me a great deal more awareness about what was beginning to happen in my country. Still at that time, public knowledge and talk of the war was rare. Most people did not know that there existed refugee camps in El Salvador such as the one I found myself working at. The only discernible and constant voice that we heard speaking out about the growing problems facing our country was that of Monsignor Oscar A. Romero.

As an ardent Catholic and a long time follower of Catholic theological teachings, I was a regular listener of Monsignor Romero's Sunday homilies at the National Cathedral. I vividly remember that, around this time, me and other young progressive people would build our personal and study schedules around the Sunday homilies delivered by Monsignor Romero at the cathedral. Monsignor Romero's insights raised our awareness and also our will to resist what was beginning to come about at the direction of government leaders and right-wing vigilantes. In the course of time, the Monsignor would be assassinated precisely for having had the courage to speak out against the injustices that were emerging all around us. Monseñor Romero left an indelible mark in my soul that lives in me to this date.

Those of us left behind who were in a position to protest were becoming more and more fearful for our own safety. There was a generalized psychosis developing in El Salvador, a manifestation of the psychological war those interested in preserving the status quo were then seeking to impose on us. Their aim was to paralyze dissent through fear. This was the period in which people who had dared to challenge the powers that be were appearing decapitated in the streets; when teachers and professors were being kidnapped from schools and colleges, never to be seen again; when, after midnight, security forces and death squads would randomly target innocents and terrorize entire families or young people.

I had friends and acquaintances who were part of the guerrilla resistance movement that was the target of government and right-wing reaction during these years. They would talk to me about the unspeakable horrors that were unfolding all around us. Their recounts of the atrocities that were beginning to occur reinforced in many of us the sense of psychosis, fear and insecurity that was becoming dominant in our conscience. We were all left with a clear sense of not being free or safe.

This environment of fear was far-reaching and impossible to ignore. My family was directly affected by it too. I remember one day, for example, around this time when I was talking to my mother and she surprised me with a desperate plea and a rush of tears. I had never seen my mother cry, as she is a very strong woman; but through her tears she implored me to make a promise to her. Her specific request was, "Don't get involved with the guerrilla fighters." I tried to downplay her grounds for concern but she was compelled to go further. "Don't become a guerilla," she pressed me, "because the day that you do, I will die."

My mother's words penetrated me like a laser. Her fear and love for me were both powerfully evident. Perhaps her emotional admonition not to join the resistance was my mother's way of blackmailing me or merely pre-empting an unlikely but nevertheless terrifying possibility; but, in the situation at that moment in time, both she and I had grounds to be fearful. I was a young medical student attending the Universidad Nacional, which was being heavily persecuted by the government as a place of subversion. I had already brushed up against several dangerous encounters with the authorities that could have put me at great risk of injury or death. All around us, moreover, there were growing signs that the situation in our nation was becoming grave. So I made a promise to my mother that I would not become an armed guerilla fighter.

I frankly did not know if I could fulfill this promise to my mother, but I felt I owed it to her to try my best to do so. She had dedicated her entire life to me and our broad extended family. It had cost her a lot, and I felt that accommodating her request to stay out of the armed resistance movement was something concrete that I could do for her, to honor her many sacrifices over the years.

Some time shortly after the conversation with my mother about staying out of the violence, when I was back working at San José de la Montaña seminary, I lost a friend, Miguel. He had frequently traveled between San Miguel and San Salvador. At the time of his death, he had been working at the Clínica de AGEUS. One day, he did not come back to the clinic to take up his work shift. It was after he had spent the weekend at home with his family. I thought it was strange because he was very dedicated and responsible. We later learned that he had been killed.

Miguel's family owned land, had properties and hired *campesinos*. We were told that his father had gone to pick him up at the bus terminal to take him home. On the way back, the father and son were stopped at a security checkpoint. From there, it appears, they were kidnapped and murdered by paramilitary forces. This really affected me in a powerful way. It made me reflect on the possibility that the growing conflict in El Salvador had virtually no logic nor reason. Miguel came from a hardworking family. They were middle class. They were not involved in politics.

Within the next several weeks, the government closed the university. I was not there on that day; I was studying with a friend because we were going to take an important exam that afternoon. When we were ready to head to the campus at about one o'clock in the afternoon, another classmate called us and told us not to go to the university because it had been taken over by the military. There was little certainty about how long the university would be closed, but we were led to believe that it could be anywhere between two and six months. To keep myself involved in productive activities during this time, I started working at a local store and I continued to go to San José de la Montaña.

Two of my co-workers at San José de la Montaña received anonymous phone threats during this period. I did not get any calls like the ones they got, but with everything that was going on, my friend Miguel's murder, Monsignor Romero's assassination, the university closing, etc., I felt that the instability overtaking El Salvador was reaching crisis proportions. More and more innocent people seemed to be getting wrapped up in the madness. My strong and growing sense of this culminated when one of my best friend's mothers, a very nice and stable woman, was kidnapped from the school where she taught. They took her in the middle of the day, in broad daylight. She was never seen again.

With these developments I began to look for a way out of El Salvador. It was unsafe to be there. I wanted to study English. I knew that it would help me in my career, because all the books and articles me and my medical school classmates were reading in our university courses were in English. So my mother suggested that I go study with a friend's daughter in Mississippi. The friend's daughter had been sent by her family to Hattiesburg, Mississippi to study English at the university located there. We researched the possibilities of my gaining admission to the U.S. school and my mom said, "With some effort, we can do it." Indeed, I was eventually admitted to the school. I arrived in southern Mississippi in late October of 1980. I was very lucky because when I asked for a student visa, U.S. authorities in El Salvador gave it to me. I arrived via New Orleans and that is how my life here in the United States began.

Upon arrival, one of the first things I did out of necessity, as well as a fortuitous tip from an acquaintance, was to seek legal asylum status. I got the idea from a young man I met who had been in Mississippi for three years. When he learned that I too was from El Salvador, he told me, "Man, Salvadorans are getting political asylum really easily these days," which in reality was a big misunderstanding of the political asylum process that at the time used to grant work permits to all applicants, but actual asylum to only a few. I immediately contacted three or four Salvadorans whom I knew were residing in town and we all started talking and meeting. There were so few of us in the region; even now, there are not many Salvadorans in Mississippi. The young man who gave me the early tip to seek asylum then helped all of us through the process. We went to see a notary and completed lots of paperwork. Then we all traveled to San Francisco where U.S. authorities would review and decide on our applications.

We left on a Wednesday night and got there on Thursday. Later that day we had our appointment. We sought official political asylum status in the United States. The friend who coached us through it all submitted our paperwork. Within a couple of short hours we were done. On that same day, we received work permits. It was really easy for us. Back in Mississippi, we applied for and quickly got social security cards. I began to take more English classes, two in my first semester of study. Each one lasted eight weeks. During this period the 1981 offensive was getting started in El Salvador. It made me reflect on the worsening situation of my country. I thought about my mother and realized that with El Salvador's worsening economic health (as a result of the war), she would have a hard time paying for my tuition.

Suddenly, studying did not seem like the best thing for me. The circumstances of the moment called on me to do something substantially different than what I was doing. I had friends in Los Angeles with whom I shared my predicament during a phone call. They offered me a place to stay in their home. So I moved to Los Angeles and lived with them for a time. The first thing that I did was to find a job. I found work on my very first day there. It was not difficult at that time to find employment. The English that I had studied and learned over the years helped me a lot. I also had a girlfriend who had come before me to Los Angeles, so we saw each other again and she helped me a great deal to make the transition to life in southern California. My friend was a very socially active person, though not involved in any particular political group. She came from a family with a strong political consciousness.

Shortly after we became reconnected in Los Angeles my friend told me, "There's going to be an event this weekend and Mejía Godoy—a Nicaraguan musician—will be there." I think it was Carlos Mejía Godoy. She wanted me to go to this gathering. The event was to be at a church that no longer exists, a Methodist church then known as the First Methodist Church of Los Angeles. The church was housed in a building that was an old-fashioned, gothic-type structure. At the event that my friend encouraged me to attend, I met many people working in the then-emerging Solidarity Movement. Among this clustering of people located at the church's entrance was a solidarity group known as the Ernesto Jovel committee. I eventually found my way to this group's conversation and by the time we all said goodbye, I had been invited to participate with them in an important activity. That Sunday all of us would celebrate the anniversary of Monsignor Oscar A. Romero's death.

The celebration was at Saint Francis Church in Los Angeles near the city's Garment District. My girlfriend and I attended and along the way I unexpectedly ran into an old classmate, Humberto, from the university in San Salvador. He told me he was involved in some important solidarity organizing activities through the Ernesto Jovel Committee. He invited to become active as well. His engagement in this work and his endorsement of the others participating in it gave me the confidence to join up and get involved later on. At that time. I knew virtually nothing about the Ernesto Jovel Committee, and, except for my friend from El Salvador, I did not know any of the people involved.

Humberto really encouraged me. "Come to the meetings," he told me. "We meet on Sundays and we have activities, like raffles for solidarity in El Salvador." His encouragements found a receptive ear. As an immigrant, you miss your country a lot, especially when you leave in the kind of situation in which many of us from El Salvador had to. You worry about what is going on back home, and in our case we could never get away from it. News on El Salvador and the growing violence and death there appeared nearly every day on U.S. television and in the leading newspapers. Involvement in groups like the Ernesto Jovel Committee gave asylum seekers like me the opportunity to stay connected to what was happening in El Salvador. We wanted to remain in touch with and supportive of our loved ones and friends who stayed behind; and we also felt special pressures to be actively involved in supporting our country's welfare.

Many of us who had found our way to places like Los Angeles felt very guilty because we knew we were relatively safer than many in our home nation; even if we now suffered economic hardships as a result of our relative poverty in America, we were safe from intimidation, torture and death. So, a heightened feeling of responsibility and a lingering sense of guilt motivated me to participate in the Ernesto Jovel Solidarity Committee. The group's activities were primarily cultural. We had assemblies on Sundays and watched television news clips of what was happening in El Salvador. We benefited from many cultural and artistic presentations featuring musicians who created wonderful music and camaraderie. Although most of us were barely getting to know each other, there was a feeling of solidarity with other people that the committee's work helped to create for our budding community of exiles. We had a little bit of everything going on in our newly forming society. There were Salvadorans who had lived in the United States for many years such as Julio, Roberto and Chabelita. There were also many people who had only recently arrived such as Luis, Chepe, Don José, Ricardo, Jesús to mention a few. Others fell somewhere in between these extremes.

During this time, I ran into still another old friend from the university in El Salvador who had been my neighbor, Milagro. She eventually became my partner and the mother of my children. Our expanding work in the community to support one another and our families and friends in El Salvador created increasingly strong bonds between us. Another phase in my life thus began as a result of my engagement with the Ernesto Jovel Solidarity Committee. People who worked with various churches were a central part of the solidarity committee, and they were increasingly helping us organize refugee community services projects.

Over the next couple of years, into the mid-1980s, there was a sudden huge wave of Salvadorans entering the United States with a lot of challenges in front of them—legal, economic, health-related, etc. Some of my friends were already getting involved with El Rescate, which was founded in 1981, and they were working hard to address the urgent legal needs of Salvadorans seeking, as we had, official political asylum rights. They invited me to participate in El Rescate activities, to raise funds as a volunteer. We decided to organize solidarity activities in the United States. We went on an artistic tour that was organized by Casa El Salvador and visited many universities across the country. At each venue, we played music and spoke about the issues affecting El Salvador. At our events, Gavino Palomares, a Mexican musician, played and I presented for Casa El Salvador. Our efforts raised a lot of awareness in this country about the El Salvador war; it also inspired a lot of solidarity for the Salvadoran people at important U.S. colleges and universities.

Prior to the tour, I had found employment at a hospital in Los Angeles as a nurse aide. To perform on the college road tour I had asked for permission to take a three-week leave of absence from the hospital, which my employer granted me. Unfortunately, due to unanticipated demand, our college tour lasted more than a month and a half. When I returned to Los Angeles to resume my position as a nurse aide, I no longer had a job. So I started to look for another job and fortunately I found one at another area hospital. Shortly thereafter, El Rescate received funds to employ social workers as part of a California Council of Churches program that also enabled the organization to provide legal immigration aid to political asylum applicants. People came to El Rescate in huge numbers to seek this help; but they also came with many other kinds of problems related to housing, work, health and other issues they were facing. El Rescate decided to create a social services department and since I knew English more or less and had been active and effective in my voluntary work for the agency, they asked me to apply for the new department's supervisory position. I got hired and I was very interested and pleased to accept such an important new job.

The new opportunity presented by El Rescate effectively closed the doors on my future in El Salvador. Simultaneous events back home would make this clear in the coming weeks. At that time, in the midst of the violence that was overtaking El Salvador, a private university had recently opened a new school of medicine, the second one in the history of El Salvador. Many of the professors from Universidad Nacional, which was still closed as a result of government intervention, had founded the new medical school. The new school's dean was a long time acquaintance of my mother, so my mother went and talked with her about me. She told the medical school dean that I had studied medicine at the Universidad Nacional and that I was living in the United States. She also asked the new dean if I could be admitted as a student to complete my studies at her school.

Following her visit to the new medical school, which I had known nothing about in advance, my mother called me on the phone to tell me that she had successfully registered me to resume my studies there. "Come back," she told me enthusiastically. "I have already registered you at the university." I was devastated. For the first time in my life, I had to tell my mother something that I knew would break her heart: "I won't go back to El Salvador," I told her. In shock, she asked why. As you can imagine, I could not easily explain it to her. She continued to press me to change my mind. In the end, I simply said no. It was one of the most painful moments of my life.

My reasons for not considering a return to El Salvador were complex. The main reason was that I was afraid of returning; I was afraid of the war. In addition, I feared that I would be marginalized back home, as I had been in the past. I dreaded the idea that I could only ever be a student in the eyes of my family and established university colleagues back home. My fear of returning to El Salvador where the armed conflict and violence were concerned was less for myself than for others. I was primarily afraid for my family's personal safety. At that time it, was not uncommon in El Salvador for entire families to suffer the consequences of the state of terror, because one member of the family was allegedly participating in revolutionary activities. I was afraid that my family might somehow have to suffer for my involvements in recent and past progressive "political" activities. I also worried about revisiting circumstances in which my own actions or those of my friends could result in death or torture. Beyond these concerns, I also resisted returning to El Salvador because, ironically, I felt that I could do more to help end the violence and injustice there from the United States.

At that point in time, a large part of what we had to do to advance justice in El Salvador involved active denunciation of what was happening there in the media and leadership circles of leading foreign nations. I felt strongly that those of us in the United States had a special responsibility to use our platform here to advocate for change in El Salvador on the world stage. I became convinced that refugees from El Salvador and other nations were the human consequence of inhumane policies. Me and my colleagues in Los Angeles had a unique opportunity to advance the strategy of denunciation and to raise essential questions such as: Why were so many Salvadorans immigrating to the United States? What were the circumstances compelling them to come here in such growing numbers? People were obviously risking a lot to migrate such a long way and under such dangerous circumstances. I felt increasingly that my work, and that of others like me, was to speak out and denounce what was generating all those refugees.

This was not an easy thing to do with success at that time. U.S. policy in El Salvador was to provide complete military and logistical support to the government. U.S. leaders did not recognize emigrating Salvadorans as refugees because doing so would have contradicted the Reagan administration's foreign policy stance. However, we knew why more and more Salvadorans and other Central Americans were streaming into the United States and we denounced it publicly. The sheer growth in the numbers of Salvadoran refugee applicants coming to the United States became a strong basis of our arguments on behalf of political asylum seekers from the region that they faced a legitimate threat of death or torture by being returned to El Salvador. While our task was not easy, in time, our U.S.-based strategy began to have a positive impact. Special status protection was applied to many refugee applicants that enabled Salvadoran refugees at risk to avoid being returned to El Salvador; moreover, important U.S. political leaders began to recognize the anti-democratic policies and practices of both the Reagan administration and Salvadoran government and vigilante leaders.

As I got more involved in the Solidarity Movement, I decided to change my name because I became afraid for my family back home. By becoming involved as a spokesperson against the Salvadoran government and its right-wing backers, I became a very public person in some respects. I received many invitations to do speaking presentations at various U.S. churches and colleges, which were very interested in El Salvador at that time. People associated with these institutions wanted to know more about what was going on and how they could become involved. In various ways, this work threatened to heighten security risks for my family back home, if my work could be traced to them in any way. This became a source of concern to me and many other U.S.-based Salvadorans who had become active in Solidarity. In fact, there were risks that we took by being involved in this work—risks that could come up in unexpected ways.

In 1983, for example, I was invited to participate in a discussion forum at Claremont College that featured not only Salvadoran anti-government advocates like me, but also two members of the ruling legislative assembly who worked closely with the very Salvadoran government leaders responsible for the violence in our country. The conversation centered on whether Salvadorans who were coming in growing numbers to the United States were economic refugees. At one point in the program, I remember that a female student asked an important if innocent question about our topic. She asked why there were so many Salvadorans who claimed they had left El Salvador for political rather than economic reasons. One of the legislative assembly leaders on the podium responded to her by saying, "That assertion is merely a fabrication of the Communists." Then, looking at me, the Salvadoran government supporter added "This man, here, is very young . . . He should be careful because he is defaming our country." Another member of the audience then stood up and asked the government spokesperson, "Are you threatening him in public?" The Salvadoran assembly leader responded, "Of course not . . ." But the hint of retaliation against me and members of my family, my friends and my associates was implicit nevertheless.

Using pseudonyms became a common practice among Salvadoran refugee leaders during the coming years, to protect ourselves and others close to us from retaliation for exercising our freedom of conscience and speech. Living this way was not easy for me. It was like experiencing schizophrenia, because in public I would use a false name, but when it came to signing official documents, I would use my real, legal name. All of my social security declarations, tax reports, etc., for example, included my real name. But in public, I became Guillermo Rodezno, a combination of the names of my best childhood friend and a prominent Salvadoran educator, and I was known as such for a very long time.

During the next several years, we continued to work very hard to secure a democratic resolution to the conflicts in El Salvador and to protect the rights and well being of Salvadoran and other Central American refugees in the United States. As time passed, our U.S.-focused community-building efforts deepened. At the beginning, we knew very little about how to position ourselves in this country. We knew little about the system or how to organize ourselves. And, yet, by staying connected to one another and by seeking the counsel of North American allies, we ultimately made major strides. That was a very interesting lesson for many of us, to discover that we could put in place a collective vision and agenda and that, after a lot of work together, we could achieve concrete gains. It was motivating to see the concepts and projects that we planned as a community finally come to fruition.

Few of us involved in this work actually made any appreciable money during these years, which makes our accomplishments all the more impressive. My salary at El Rescate, for example, was quite low and only allowed me and my family to live very modestly. Most of us involved in the early work of Solidarity worked in a collective compensation system. We had so little that the only way we could survive was literally as a community; so we established a community fund that determined how much money each of us would be paid based on a balancing of our individual and our collective needs. We agreed periodically to present personal budgets and the group of us would discuss and decide together whether each individual truly needed all the money he or she requested to live, pay rent, buy food, etc.

Looking back on these times now, it is impressive to reflect on how much work we all did for so little material compensation. We were deeply committed to our efforts for the common good of our people. There was never a time when we were not working. We worked an insurmountable amount of hours. Typically, we would start at nine in the morning and end at ten or eleven at night. We organized meetings and events every day, and our activities frequently spilled over onto Saturdays and Sundays. And yet, despite all of the hard work, this was one of the most beautiful times of my life. I think everyone involved feels the same way that I do about this, still today.

Those of us involved in this work truly came to know community, collective life in an intimate and inspiring way. We saw our efforts make a real difference in people's lives, and we developed a deep spirit of commitment. I will not call what we did a sacrifice, because it was something we did freely and with enthusiasm; but we all felt a deep commitment to selfless community work and we all gave it everything within our power to advance our cause. I remember those friends who dedicated their full time work to this cause, among them Salvador, Vladimir, Neco, Juan, Marcelo, Rolando, Francisco, Yadira and Sonia. They did not gain a secure income in doing so, and they primarily lived from week to week based on what our collective could give them. These were mainly people with families; yet they were there day and night developing projects, searching for strategies to make important contacts for us, going to meetings, organizing activities. They brought an intense focus and a lot of vision to our work. This was inspiring.

Our efforts were also significantly benefited through the hard work and generosity of committed allies within the North American community, especially some lay people such as Anne and Linda and from Protestant church groups such as Jean and Don. As a strong Catholic, I was initially shocked to find out early in our movement that, with respect to the churches, we received most of our support not from Catholic institutions, but rather from Protestant churches and networks. This reality forced me to learn about Protestant institutions and concepts in ways that ultimately helped me to grow and develop my sense of humanity. I befriended many Protestant people as a result and gained valued new insights into what is possible when we break down stereotypes and artificial divides. It was a beautiful experience, from which I learned a lot. Perhaps for the first time in my life, I truly experienced through my work with our North American Protestant allies what "solidarity" really means. As a receiver of their support and generosity, I felt a lot of solidarity with the North American people.

In subsequent years, as time has gone by, the magic of our community's initial years here has been lost and understandably so; the war is over, all of us have gone our own ways to raise families, develop careers, businesses and other interests. We have gained a lot since coming here, no doubt. Many of our people have become successful professionals, we have built important institutions, and we have learned to operate effectively within the American political system, among other things. But our community organizations do not have the same magic today as they did when we first came here, I suppose this is the logical evolution of all institutions. They do not have the same commitment or focus. I believe this is a normal development process for our community and our organizations. But I remember the work, the meetings, the events and presentations of our time with a lot more affection, perhaps even with nostalgia for the youth and idealism of that era. We were overflowing with youth and energy. Most of us were barely twenty then and thought we could change the world, or at least El Salvador.

Something particularly incredible about our experience in those years was the lack of self-interest in the majority of our people. We did not do the work of protest organizing and institution-building for a material personal gain; on the contrary, we all lost material standing by being involved in the movement. But we shared an incredible desire to do something, to add our grain of sand for social progress in any way we could. I think we had a greater awareness of what it meant to be Salvadorans, whether in El Salvador or here in the United States. Our motivation, spirit and camaraderie were incredible. With our North American allies, we created an impressive degree of international empathy, understanding and affection. All of this enabled us to accomplish great things at an important moment in our community's evolution.

When I worked at El Rescate, there were two immediate needs in the Salvadoran refugee community that outpaced all others; one was housing and the other was medical care. El Rescate and its North American supporters and allies aggressively responded to these needs. The first thing that we did was to create El Refugio (The Refuge), which was a shelter for Central American refugees. We housed homeless men and women there, as well as needy families with children, too. With a lot of work, we outfitted it nicely and made it a safe shelter for our clients. El Refugio functioned for many years and helped hundreds of Salvadoran families through some of their most difficult times.

The other project we created was the Clínica Msr. Oscar A. Romero, a community health care facility that continues to operate effectively to the present. Clínica Romero was the product of organized work in the community, and it was us, we, the refugees, who created it. I remember at that time the Santana Chirino Amaya Refugee Committee had just been formed. It carried the name of the first Salvadoran who had been deported from the United States back to El Salvador in the early 1980s and who, within days of being returned, was assassinated. To honor that individual and to raise awareness about the lingering danger that others deported could also end up dead back in El Salvador, we named the committee after Santana Chirino Amaya. The Santana Chirino Amaya Committee included people who had been working as volunteers near El Rescate. They were mainly involved in community organizing efforts to meet the people's growing needs. Some of these same people became centrally involved in developing Clínica Romero.

People sometimes ask me now, even years after my departure from El Rescate, "Why does Clínica Romero have to be involved in community-organizing work if it's a clinic that offers medical services; what does it have to do with organizing?" Well, I reply that Clínica Romero would not be here had it not been for community-organizing efforts. The community identified a need and worked to fill that void through efforts of committed volunteers, outside people with knowledge and resources, and others. Now nearly twenty-five years after Clínica Romero was founded, it is impressive to see what it has become. It houses a community health center. It is recognized and supported by the city, state, county and federal governments; and it has received support from major foundations and individual donors for its three locations. It employs some one hundred and fifty professionals, including physicians, dentists, psychologists and other health providers. It serves more that 17,000 patients a year and provides over

60,000 visits. We never imagined that the Clínica Romero would be where it is now. If someone were to have told me when we established the clinic, "In twenty-three years we will have three locations, a multi-million dollar budget and employ over one hundred people," I would have laughed out loud.

Looking at the past decades since we came to this country as Salvadoran refugees, I think it is clear that our efforts have rendered a lot of community and public benefits all across California and the hemisphere. We must not lose sight that anything that betters the lives of Salvadorans and Central Americans in this country—through their immigration status, social services, employment, housing, healthcare and so on—adds value and benefit to people here in Los Angeles, and also to their family members and the society in El Salvador.

Remittances to El Salvador from Salvadorans working and living in the United States now exceed the level of annual development assistance provided by the United States to El Salvador. Such private funding support to communities and individuals in turn serves as an important source of economic and political stability in El Salvador. It provides needed employment, human services and sustenance financing to Salvadorans of all ages. It furthermore establishes a bridge that connects Salvadorans here and there in enduring and still-critically important ways. Remittances thus serve as a vital form of transnational community building that is ultimately important for regional stability, international commerce and cultural continuity.

I feel that my efforts and those of others to facilitate peace and community building for the people of El Salvador, both back home and here in our adopted land, have been important and meaningful. Every now and then, I am reminded that our relentless work in the early years mattered. Recently, for example, I went with my children to a park here in Los Angeles and we were playing when a middle-aged man came up to me and said, "You're Guillermo, right?" I started to laugh because he used one of my aliases from the past and he said, "From the minute I saw you, I recognized you, I knew your name." I replied, "Yes, I'm Guillermo." He then said, "Do you remember me?" I did. It was a very moving encounter. I had been able to assist this person when we were both young men many years ago. I introduced him to my children, and he said to them, "I want to tell you what your dad did for me." He then explained that when he first came to Los Angeles, he did not have a place to live, or a job to earn any money. He told my children that, through my work at El Rescate, I had assisted him to find a life here, to gain housing and employment, access to quality healthcare and obtain an insight into the American political system. He now was in a better situation as a result of all that. I was deeply gratified to be reminded by this man in the presence of my children that some things I did along my journey in this country made that sort of difference in someone's life.

Msr. Oscar A. Romero, 1980. Donated to Clínica Romero in 2000.

Press conference to denounce detention centers: (from right to left) Adelfo Martínez, Francisco Rivera, Isabel Cárdenas, Alicia Rivera and Hugo Rugamas in Los Angeles, 1981.

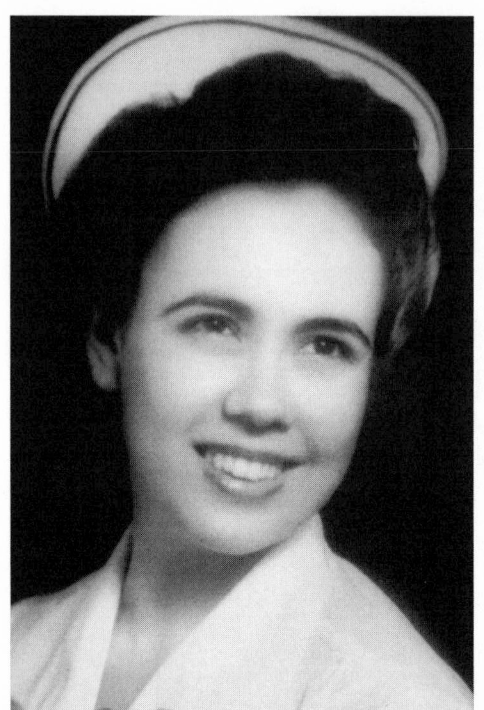

Aurora Martínez, one of the founder's of Clínica Msr. Oscar A. Romero, 1983.

First site for Clínica Msr. Oscar A. Romero, 1833 W. Pico Blvd., Los Angeles, 1983.

Santana Chirino Amaya members and Central American Refugee Committee, CRECE, hunger strike in Placita Olvera Street Church, Rossana Pérez (third from right) Los Angeles, 1983.

First location of the Central American Refugee Committee, CRECE, in Bonnie Brae, Los Angeles, 1983.

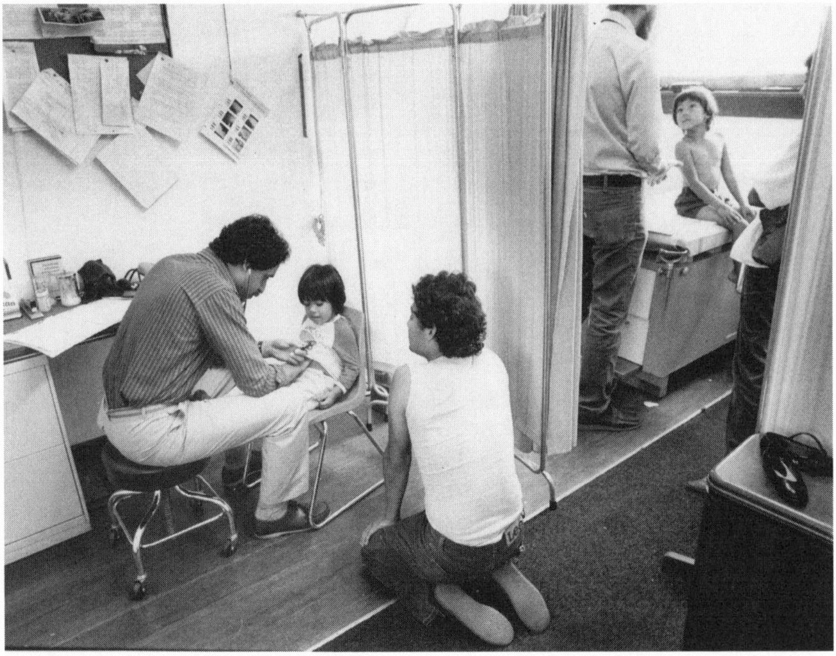

Pediatricians providing care at Clínica Msr. Oscar A. Romero, Los Angeles, 1983.

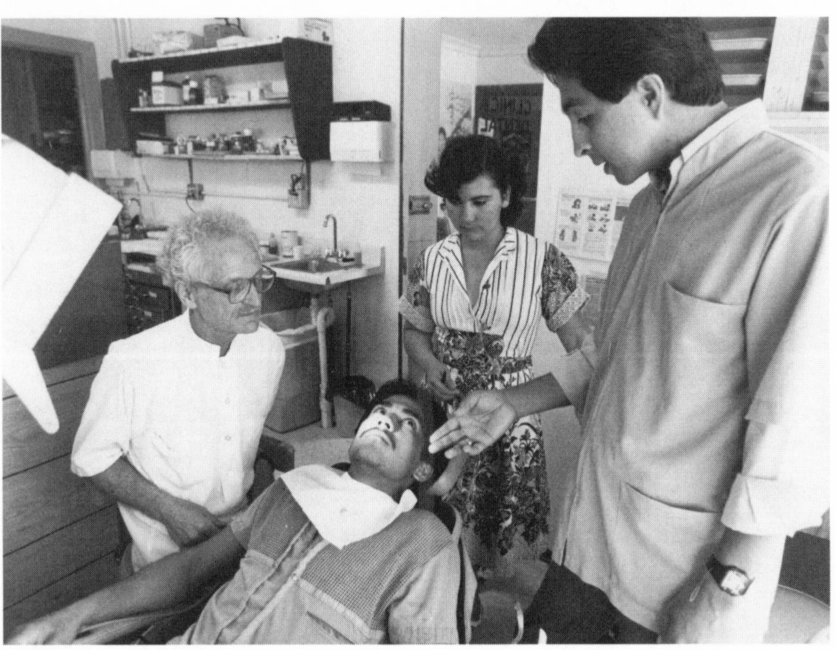

Dr. Hoffman (sitting); Dr. Mercedes Mendoza, dental clinic coordinator; patient and translator at Clínica Msr. Romero, Los Angeles, 1984.

Press conference for political asylum at CARECEN: Sandra Petit, attorney, El Rescate; Linton Joaquin, attorney, CARECEN; Father Mike Kennedy, Placita Olvera Street Church; Hugo Rugamas, El Rescate; Jesús Aguilar, Refugee Committee; and members of a family living in sanctuary, Los Angeles, 1984.

Son and father reunion after the boy's liberation from the "El Centro" detention center, Los Angeles, 1984.

A Way of Hope SCARC

The Santana Chirino Amaya Refugee Committee, named after a Salvadoran who was deported from the United States and found decapitated in El Salvador a month later, was formed in 1981 by a group of refugees bonded out of detention for the purpose of organizing the refugee community. They work closely with El Rescate and are currently helping their brothers and sisters, displaced by the air war and military operations, repopulate their towns.

La Clinica Msr. Romero:

Named for the Roman Catholic archbishop of El Salvador who was murdered by a death squad in 1980, La Clinica provides medical care to newly arrived Central American refugees. Many suffer both the physical and psychological traumas of those who have lived through war and a lifetime of poverty. Intestinal parasites, tuberculosis, diabetes and hypertension are just a few of the problems we commonly treat.

The clinic's services include:
*Preventive screening and diagnostic testing
*Immunizations
*Pediatric, adult medical and gynecological screening, diagnosis and treatment
*Dental care
*Nutrition and health education counseling
*An extensive medical referral system.

Virtually all the supplies, equipment and medication used by La Clinica have been donated. More than 50 doctors, nurses and medical technicians volunteer their services.

For more information (213) 389-0288 1833 W. Pico Blvd. L.A., CA 90006

Angelino Landscape

I left my apartment
and walked down Alvarado
without a destination
ignoring the traffic signals
telling me: "Don't Walk"

I saw
the cocacola stained sidewalks,
the filthy hamburger smog,
the coming and going of the schizophrenic
sirens of the fire truck,
the cancerous busses,
the chaotic cars

I saw
the prostitutes make-up
the shivering of the hungry
the Salvadoran's hanging out,
the organic unemployment
the friendly drug connection,

I saw
the piles of trash
the raging ambulances flying past.
the piss on the cantina walls
the junk food stands,
the magazine stands offering
anti-culture

I saw
the claustrophobia between buildings

the drunken drifters
the cement jungle
the racist grimaces of the police,
in MacArthur Park,
the Third World,
"Little Central America,"
the eye for an eye of survival,
the tooth for a tooth of the next
step forward...
my head aches from walking
without a destination.

I see my face reflected
in the shop window faces
of my Central American brother
who are also walking without a
destination, ignoring the nagging
of the traffic signals
that say: "Don't Walk."

Clínica Msr. Romero and Santana Chirino Amaya Refugee Committee information flyer for the community, Los Angeles, 1984.

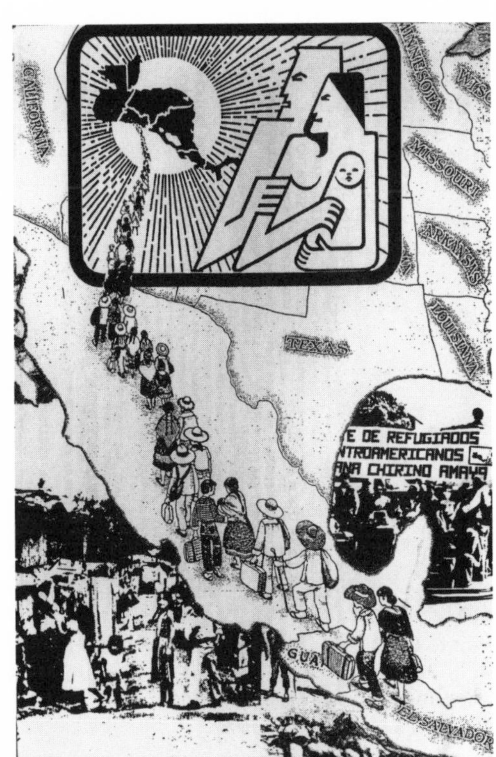

Artwork by Ricardo García O'mainey used in publications by the Santana Chirino Amaya Refugee Committee, Los Angeles, 1984.

Anne Mello receives the first grant for Clínica Msr. Oscar A. Romero, Los Angeles, 1984

Visit to Clínica Msr. Oscar A. Romero by Los Angeles mayor Tom Bradley; Anne Mello, director; Dr. Jack Kent, medical director; Debbie Benada, R.N.; and E. Valentino, BOD president. Javier Huete and his daughter Celeste are standing by the door, Los Angeles, 1985.

Members of the Sanctuary Movement and supporters of the Central American community in Los Angeles. Gloria Kinsler, Coordinator of Southern California Eunemical Council Interfaith Task Force on Central America (SCITCA); Robert Foxworth, actor; Michael Woo, councilmember; Mike Farrel, actor and SCITCA member; and sister Joan de Quatro, 1985.

Susan Kandel with donations for earthquake victims in El Salvador. El Rescate, Los Angeles, 1986.

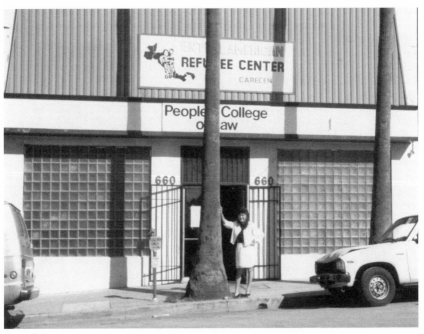

CARECEN building on Bonnie Brae, Los Angeles, 1986.

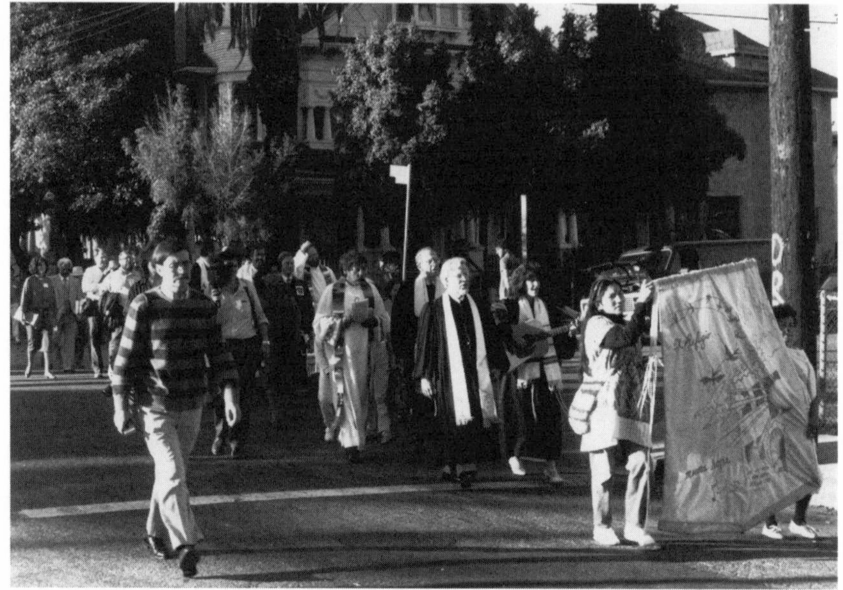

Procession of representatives from various religious denominations and the community to inaugurate El Refugio (The Shelter), Los Angeles, 1986. Rossana Pérez is holding the banner on the left.

Community demonstration at MacArthur Park, Los Angeles, 1986.

Rossana Pérez packing food for the distribution at El Refugio, Los Angeles, 1986.

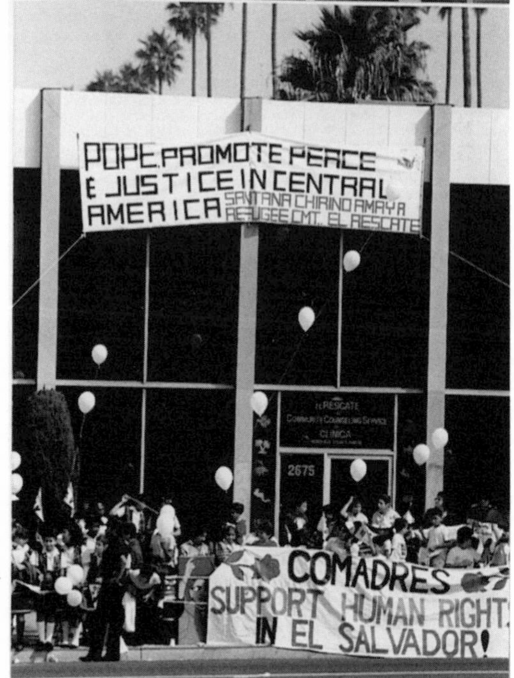

Community gathers with banners to petition for support from Pope John Paul II in Central American peace process, Los Angeles, 1987.

El Rescate

A PROJECT OF THE SOUTHERN CALIFORNIA ECUMENCIAL COUNCIL

Clínica Msr. Romero

Volume 5 Issue 2 2675 WEST OLYMPIC BOULEVARD, LOS ANGELES, CA 90006 September, 1987

The Prospect for Peace in Central America

The most promising peace plan for Central America, announced in August, came not from Washington but from Central America itself. No one who believes in the fundamental principle of self-determination should be surprised. All five Central American Presidents signed the agreement, calling for amnesty to insurgents, dialogue with unarmed opposition, an end to the states of emergency, free elections under existing constitutions, and a ban on outside aid to insurgents. Given the Reagan Administration's preoccupation with Nicaragua, most media attention has focused on the plan's effect on that nation. Little press attention has been given to the plan's effects in El Salvador and Guatemala.

Rather than directly address the social conditions that caused the wars, the plan provides a forum in each country for the internal opposition to raise the important issues. In El Salvador, many provisions of the plan hold little promise. The relatively self sufficient FMLN guerrillas are not vulnerable to an aid cutoff, and a successful amnesty program is unlikely, given the rapidly deteriorating human rights situation. With hundreds of millions of dollars in aid, El Salvador's armed forces have little incentive to negotiate a cease fire, and are busy pursuing a military victory. In fact, El Rescate's Human Rights Department has received a surge of reports of abuses since the signing of the agreement.

But the fact that Duarte has endorsed the Arias plan is itself a good sign. Under pressure from Reagan, Duarte had blocked past proposals. Duarte's endorsement is further evidence that his relations with the Administration have soured recently: For over a year, U.S. aid to El Salvador has been limited to military assistance. With no economic aid, domestic opposition to Duarte has ballooned, as has military repression. While the Arias plan provides some

(continued page three)▶

Edificio Romero Opens

History was made on July 25th when El Rescate and the Clinica "Monseñor Oscar Romero" moved with Community Counseling Service/Amanecer program into new offices at the Edificio Romero. The opening of services in our new quarters marks the culmination of a year-long campaign of cooperative planning, fundraising, design and construction. Edificio Romero exemplifies the word "community," a celebration of the untiring work of our volunteers and the generous contributions of our friends and supporters. We, and all of you who worked so hard to make this move a reality, have much to be proud of.

With extensive rehabilitation work needed, a creative and cooperative fundraising strategy was developed. At the initiation of CCS, the three-agency rehabilitation project received capital grants from the ARCO and the Ahmanson Foundations; CCS was awarded a generous matching grant from the Weingart Foundation.

In order to meet the grant challenge, El Rescate began a building campaign mail fund to all its supporters. To date, El Rescate has raised $27,000 in pledges and contributions which reflect the support of hundreds of people in the community.

Clinica Board member Tina Martinez secured the invaluable assistance of AFL-CIO trade unionists, who donated their time, skills and materials in all areas of construction to transform a run-down, abandoned bank building into our bustling new quarters. Tina recently hosted a thank-you celebration fiesta to honor and thank these special supporters, including Elmer Griggs, who supervised the rehabilitation construction, Bill Robertson of the Los Angeles County Federation of Labor (AFL-CIO), Dick Sprague of the International Brotherhood of Electrical Workers, and many others who worked so hard on the reconstruction of the Edificio Romero.

Special thanks also go to architects John Silber and Robert Bickel of the L.A. Community Design Center who worked against all odds to meet each agency's needs with limited resources and space. And let's not forget the work of our dedicated staff and volunteers who, with the help of the Delancey Street Movers, packed, moved and unpacked in only two days, turning a potential catastrophe into a smooth and joyful experience for all.

The culminating celebration, our joint building dedication, was held on October 7. We were pleased to have officials such as Deputy Mayor Grace Davis, County Supervisors Edmund Edelman and Kenneth Hahn, State Assembly-man Tom Hayden, and others join us as we dedicated our new offices. Our thanks to all who made our move possible! ■

Photo printed of Pope John Paul II passing before Clínica Msr. Romero, Los Angeles, 1987.

Ana Friendly, former director of Clínica Msr. Oscar A. Romero with Eduardo González and staff, Los Angeles, 1988.

Poetry reading with Ricardo Garcia O'mainey, Sonia Baires, Alfonso Quijada Urias, Rossana Pérez, Raymundo Reynoso and Francis Rivera, Los Angeles, 1988.

CARECEN on Bonnie Brae St., Los Angeles, 1988.

Clínica Msr. Oscar A. Romero staff: Oscar López, Blanca Orellana and Mario Hernández, Los Angeles, 1989.

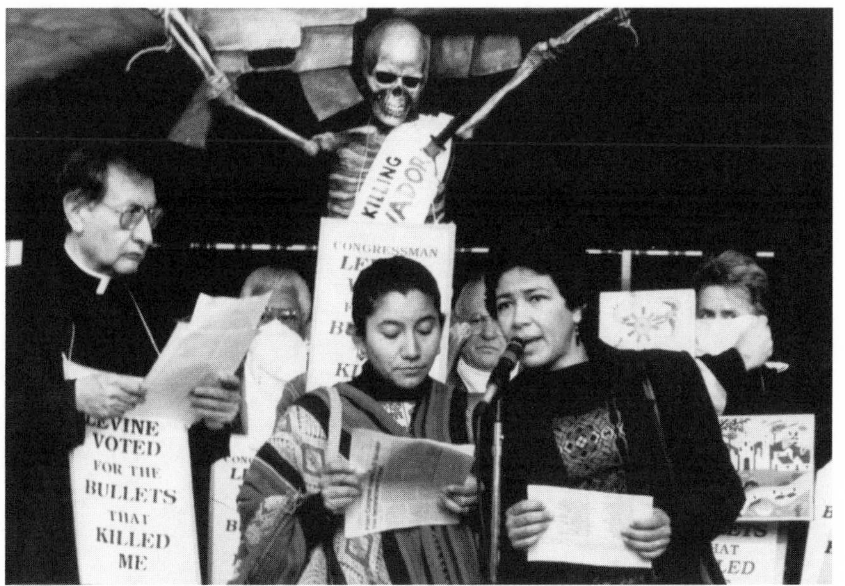

Father Luis Olivares, Placita Olvera Street Church, Rossana Pérez, Santana Chirino Amaya Refugee Committee, and Ana Castillo, CARECEN, at Sanctuary demonstration at the Federal Building in downtown, Los Angeles, 1989.

Members of the Sanctuary Movement protesting the assassination of Jesuit priests, downtown, Los Angeles, 1989.

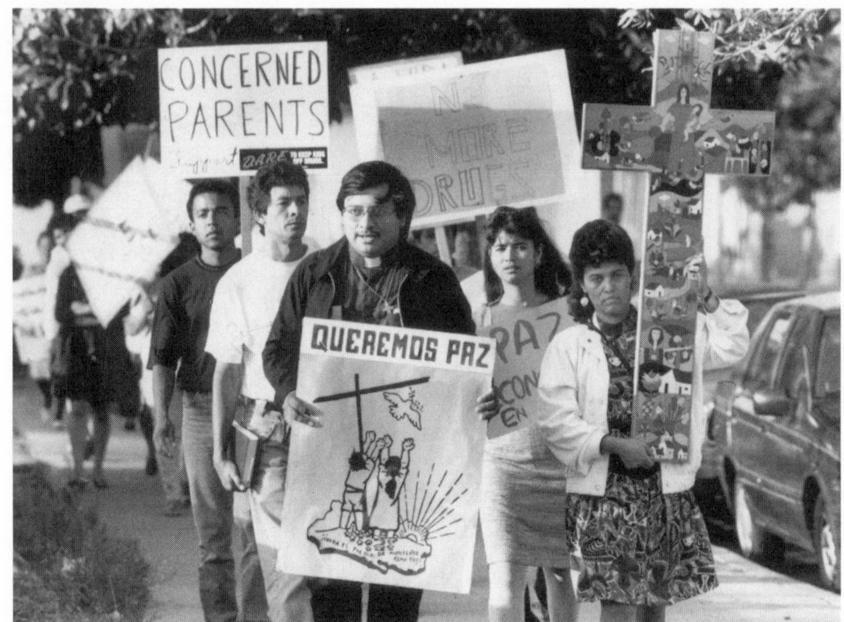

Demonstration for peace in El Salvador, Pastor Tomás López from United Methodist Church, Los Angeles, 1990.

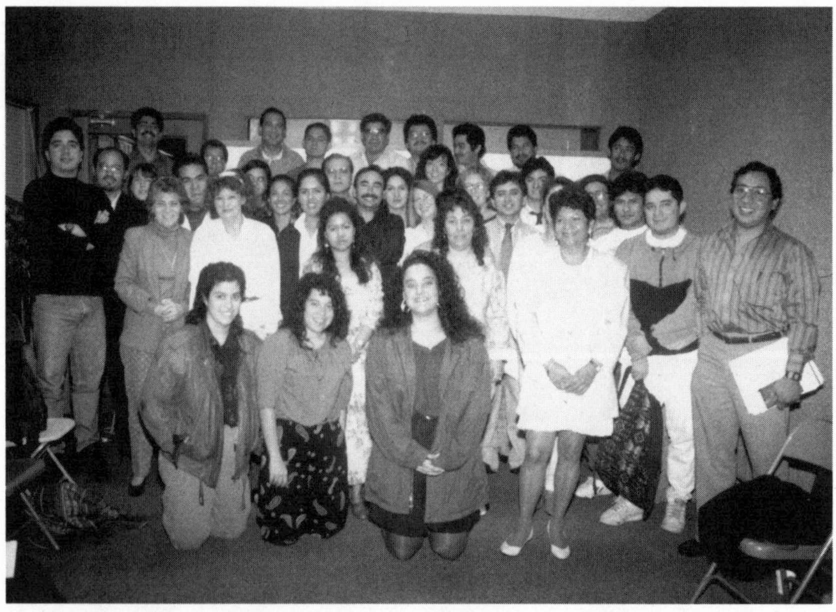

CARECEN staff and Board of Directors, Isabel Beltrán Orantes (first row, standing), Los Angeles, 1992.

Community demonstration to support amnisty, Los Angeles, 1992.

Community party to support Street Vendor Association, Dora Alicia Alarcón (president), Los Angeles, 1992.

Liberty Hill Foundation (LHF) at the Upton Sinclair Award Dinner: Sarah Pillsbury, LHF founder with honorees Robin Canon, Rossana Pérez, Bonnie Raitt, David Cleannon and Jackson Browne, Los Angeles, 1992.

Community meeting at CARECEN with Angela Zambrano and Javier Huete (far right), Los Angeles, 1993.

Community demonstration in Los Angeles, Jorge Rivera and Isabel Beltrán Orantes, 1994.

Community and government representatives with Carlos Vaquerano (right) and Councilmen Ed Reyes, Los Angeles, 1994.

Isabel Beltrán Orantes speaking at community gathering at MacArthur Park, Los Angeles, 1996.

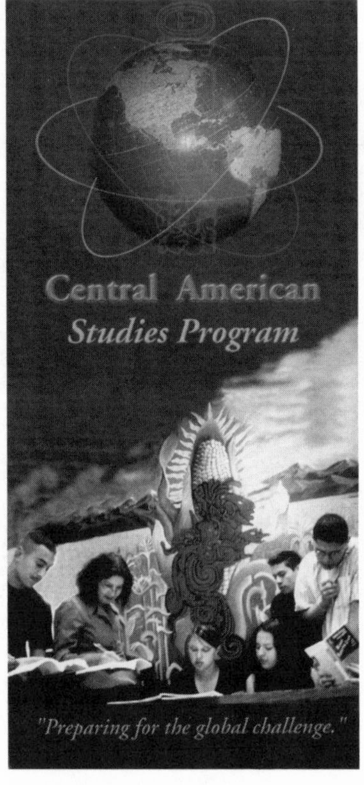

Brochure to promote the Central American Studies Program at Cal State University, Northridge, 1999. Siris Barrios (standing) with members of Central American Students Association (CAUSA).

CARECEN building on Seventh St., Los Angeles, 1999.

CARECEN Annual dinner: Douglas Carranza, Aquiles Magaña, Joaquín Chávez, Roberto Lovato, Central American Studies Program Coordinator at CSUN, and Channel 34 representative, Los Angeles, 2000.

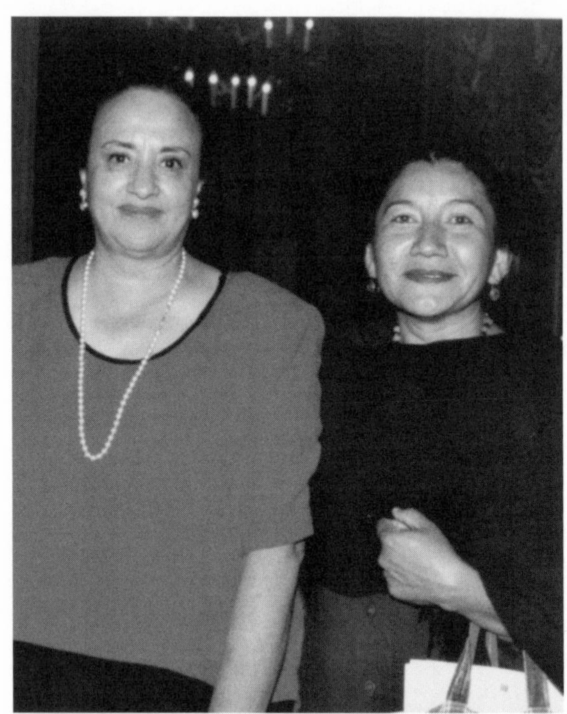

Angela Zambrano and Rossana Pérez at CARECEN Annual dinner, Los Angeles, 2000.

The Coalition for Human Immigrant Rights in Los Angeles, 2000. Day Labor Workers Program honored by CARECEN.

Community demostration to support legalization of immigrants, City Hall, Los Angeles, 2000.

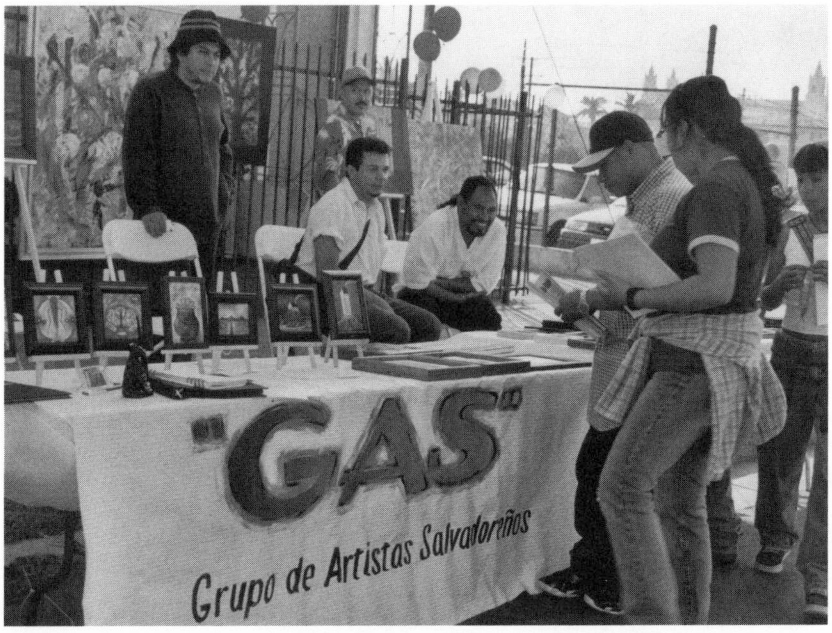

Pedro Cruz of Salvadoran Artist Group at CARECEN Street festival, Los Angeles, 2000.

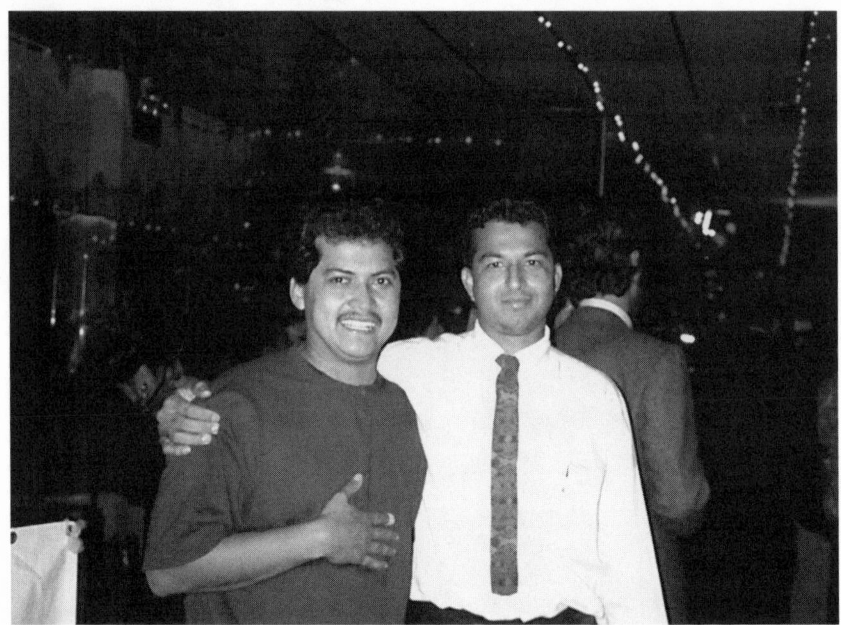

Aquiles Magaña, CARECEN board member, and Carlos Vaquerano at CARECEN Annual dinner, Los Angeles, 2001.

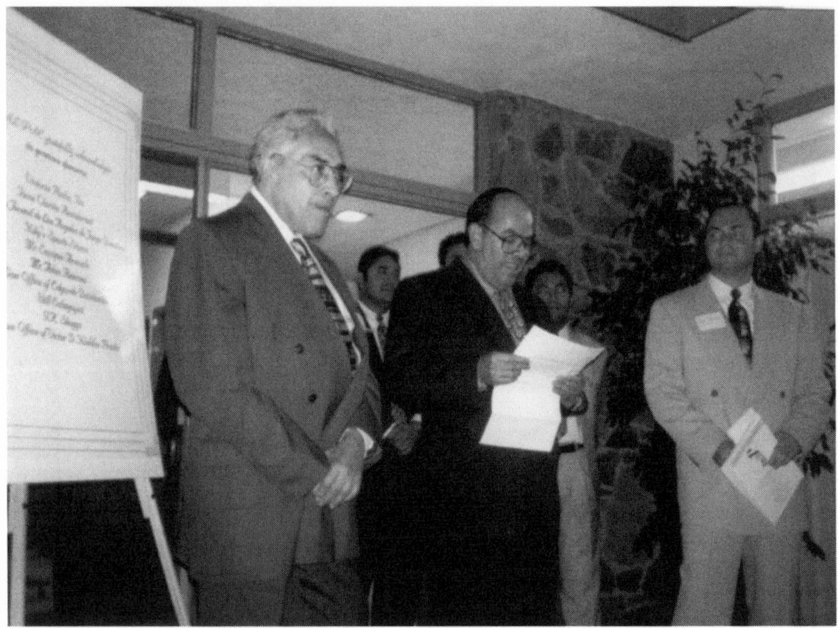

Jaime Jovel, Francisco Rivera and Randy Hurtado Ertll at CARECEN, Los Angeles, 2001.

Memorial for the fallen immigrants, Los Angeles, 2001.

March for Late Amnesty. Mayron Payes of CHIRLA (to the left) and Angela Zambrano, former CARECEN director behind the banner, Los Angeles, 2001.

Clínica Msr. Oscar A. Romero board members receive recognition in the community. Assembly member Xavier Becerra is speaking, Los Angeles, 2001.

Rossana Pérez and Angela Zambrano, CARECEN former director, Los Angeles, 2002.

CARECEN Youth Program graduates from a video class, Los Angeles, 2003.

Angela Zambrano (front row, right) with youth graduating from video class at CARECEN, Los Angeles, 2003.

Clínica Romero Community Center, Alvarado St., Los Angeles, 2003.

Children painting with Rocío Veliz at CARECEN, Los Angeles, 2003.

Angela Zambrano, former director of CARECEN, Los Angeles, 2004.

Group of children from the CARECEN afterschool program painting a mural, Los Angeles, 2004

Clínica Oscar A. Romero extension, Marengo St., Los Angeles, 2004.

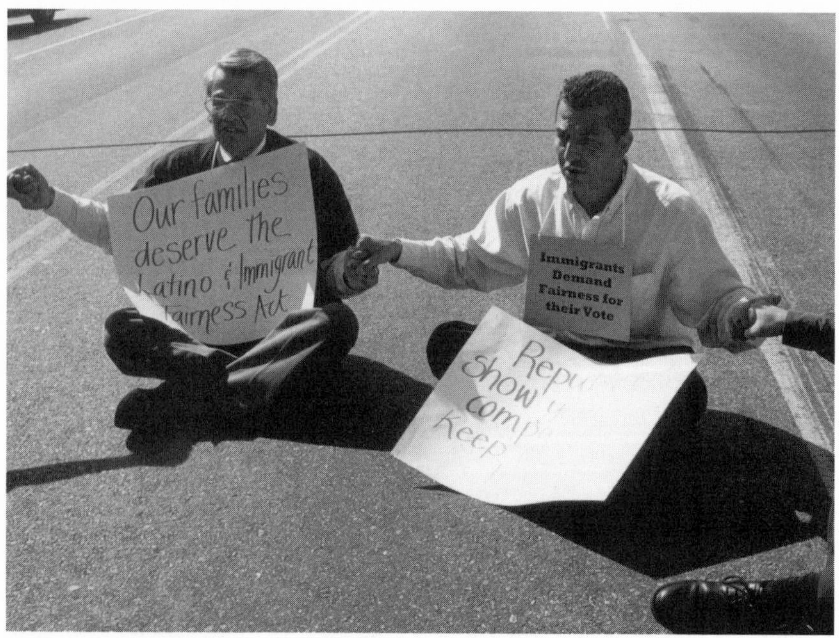

Carlos Vaquerano (right) in a street sat-down for fairness to Latino voters, Los Angeles, 2004.

Javier Huete

I was born in a town called Izalco in the county of Sonsonete in El Salvador. During my childhood I was affected by numerous things that helped to shape my journey, but I remember most my grandfather's stories. He seemed to have been especially marked by events that occurred during the 1930s, and especially the 1932 uprising of the indigenous people in El Salvador. In many cases, I recall, I would later read about the things he told me of in books on the history of El Salvador at my school. For example, he told me of how there was a massive burial of Indians in Izalco. The massacres of the Indians that took place during those years in Izalco were brutal. The Indians had no way to retaliate against the government's force, as they did not have arms.

As a result of government policy during that era, many of the nation's indigenous people became indentured farm workers. In the process, they were effectively forced to stop being Indian. They stopped speaking their languages and started speaking Spanish, however garbled. They also lost their traditional dress. That is, they stopped wearing the Indian attires that had been their standard for centuries and they started dressing like the non-Indian Salvadoran farm workers, wearing plaid shirts tied with a knot on the front, short pants, straw hats, *tecomates* and so forth. These changes had profound affects on the whole of our national culture and my grandfather made me aware of this. That is one of the things I remember from my early years.

The other thing I recall from my early years in El Salvador is that in Izalco many urban legends circulated about trips to the Atecosol Springs, Cipitio and Chillón. These legends in turn were perceived as real events in the minds of children like me. For this reason, trips to these places were initially foreboding, even though frequent. Among the things that we were told when I was young was that we could not go there alone because on the way, daunting and dangerous figures with names like La Chillona, La Cihuabana or El Cipitio were known to appear and snatch children up or do away with them altogether.

A similar recollection from my childhood is that the town of Atecosol had many images of indigenous deities and gods that no one really knew about; but they were ever present and mysterious. Still today, they are sculpted in stone and they are there, in plain view. People sit on them and sunbathe, but no one bothers to know who they are. There was also a cult in Cipitio, and an imposing sculpture there too. That is where we would go whenever we would visit. The Cipitio statue's featured figure sits above a fountain peeing. Real water literally shoots from his penis. People go see it, but they do not know what it means.

Another thing that I remember from those early days is that we were always moving because we were poor. We moved from Sonsonate to Izalco and then to San Salvador. I suppose that happens everywhere, but this kind of constant migration became very common in El Salvador because of the poverty. With every move, we would leave behind relatives, friends and school classmates that we remembered and loved in those times. But we had no choice; we had to move in order to survive.

Over the years, this kind of constant movement among the Salvadoran people became an international phenomenon. In other words, in those years, Salvadorans began no longer to move solely within our own country, but also increasingly outside of it owing initially to economic considerations. Later, with the war of the 1980s, people left the country in even greater numbers, this time primarily for political reasons. Now, as an adult, I have a clearer sense of the factors that motivated all of the movement and uprooting we experienced during my youth and young adulthood. At the time, I did not fully understand it all as I do now.

My early education is one of the reasons that I think I was able later in my life to put all of this in context. I studied during my elementary years in Izalco. I think that the basis of my educational—and, later, political—formation took root during my elementary school experience. I only had one teacher during that entire period, from first to fifth grade. She was an excellent teacher; she was very knowledgeable and knew how to transmit information and knowledge to her students. I then had another very good teacher during my sixth grade year.

I will never forget the foundation afforded to me by that early educational experience. Whenever I think about my education I always think back to my elementary years, because that is where I think I and others of my generation learned the most and where we learned and practiced a bit of discipline. In subsequent years, El Salvador's circumstances would rob its youth of education and discipline; but, during my formative years, teachers would discipline us to make us learn.

After I graduated from elementary school, I moved to San Salvador to complete middle school. Later on, I came back to Sonsonate to complete high school. After that, I spent two years traveling, mostly abroad. I traveled to Mexico, the United States and other countries. For many years, I moved around constantly like this. Events largely outside of my control mainly accounted for this.

In the years following my school completion, I married and my wife and I had our son. Shortly thereafter, we left for Mexico. We left because of the political persecution that was becoming rampant at that time. During and after my high school years, there were increasingly visible persecutions taking place in El Salvador. People were being persecuted for political, religious, race and cultural reasons. Also, if one were young and a student at the university, he or she was likely to be targeted. All of this directly affected me and my family. My parents' house was searched twice. The authorities did not find anything suspect and I do not even know to this day exactly what they were looking for. But the experience was nevertheless unsettling. Later, other family members were persecuted. I have one sister and four brothers. My older brothers were all persecuted.

My oldest brother was the first in our family to leave the country on account of these intrusions. He studied at ENCO (Escuela Nacional de Comercio), our country's leading business school. He left El Salvador following a government raid of the school, which was ostensibly considered to be harboring "subversives." He was one of the first people to be detained by the military in that instance. They suspected him and others of being or supporting communists, terrorists and other suspected "enemies of the state." They severely beat and intimidated him and he was left with a serious psychosis. He became so afraid that afterwards he could not encounter soldiers or policemen without panicking.

Following his beating at the hands of the authorities, my brother never went out alone; he was always accompanied. In time, I became most responsible for going everywhere with him to ensure his comfort and safety. After a time, he could not take it anymore and he left for the United States, to settle in Los Angeles. As the persecutions became more intense and systematic, one of my other brothers was disappeared. A person who was driving with my brother at the time he was abducted told us that the military took him along the road from San Salvador to Suchitoto. We started looking for the body; we looked everywhere from the roadside where he was taken to various tombs around the region. But we never found him.

After that, my wife began to experience official pressure. She ultimately had to seek political asylum at the Nicaraguan Embassy. She had been working with a group of students that became a target of considerable government concern during this period. In addition, during this time, one of her brothers was killed at the Universidad Nacional in the course of a heavy-handed police action. In the wake of these developments, my wife was denied asylum status by the Nicaraguans and she consequently had to leave the country via the embassy of Mexico. I accompanied her with our son. That is how we got out of El Salvador alive.

As all of this happened my remaining siblings also left El Salvador. Eventually, our whole family ended up in the United States. Ironically, years earlier, after my father passed, my mother had made her way to the States; so, she was already outside of El Salvador when the government's actions and those of right-wing vigilante groups began to result in widespread transgressions against the people. She primarily left the country because of economic reasons, becoming a so-called economic refugee during the 1970s. Her initial move was to New Orleans because work and a then-relatively large and established community of Salvadorans could be found there. But after my oldest brother made his way to Los Angeles, my mother eventually joined him.

My wife and I first came to the U.S. through Washington, DC, the capitol. We quickly found work in Washington. But we only lasted a year there and then moved to Los Angeles to join my family. Washington was cold and tedious; it is a city that is basically all about politics. At first it made sense for us to be there. We took up jobs with a Salvadoran rights group, one of the earliest of its kind to form and to inspire what later became the Solidarity and Sanctuary Movements.

My wife and I were naturally drawn to this work given the experiences that had compelled us to flee El Salvador; we wanted to do something meaningful and constructive to address the government's growing abuses. In fact, we had started to become involved in political work to end the persecution in our country by the time we ended up as exiles in Mexico. But in the United States our work on the issues intensified. In the beginning, we and others helped to form a support network of human beings—of expatriated Salvadorans and North American Anglos, that is—working on behalf of Salvadoran-based prisoners and others who were being tortured and otherwise abused. We also worked to support Salvadorans who were beginning to flee in growing numbers to Honduras when the persecution became even fiercer.

Around this time, we started talking publicly about the persecutions taking place in El Salvador, in order to educate the U.S. and world communities about what was happening there and to help put external pressure on the Salvadoran authorities. We also worked to assemble money and material goods to send to El Salvador in support of the abused and their families—things like shoes, clothes and medicines (such as antibiotics). It was all very informal, even though organized. We would send the affected parties assistance packages in the luggage of friends who would visit El Salvador periodically. We did not send things in bulk or boxes. These early efforts laid the groundwork for work that became more visible and formalized in subsequent years with the involvement of key North American religious organizations.

In Mexico, the Salvadoran rights and justice agency I worked with had mainly collected policy and strategic information of all that was happening on the issues in Washington, in El Salvador and throughout the Central American region. I would disseminate this information to Central American activists and leaders of the U.S.-Salvadoran Solidarity Movement. When I left Mexico with my family in 1983 and arrived in Washington, I almost immediately started working with the

Solidarity Movement there. Our public research and advocacy efforts were especially important in those days. Few in the United States were really aware then of Salvadorans' reasons for coming to the United States in such large and growing numbers or the role that the U.S. government had played in contributing to this exodus by either tacitly or directly supporting the Salvadoran government's persecution and bombings in the cities and the countryside of our nation.

At the time, the situation in El Salvador was not widely understood to be a civil war, but that was what it had become. In spite of this fact, the Reagan administration painted the situation as one in which outside communist forces were imposing themselves on a democracy-loving government. This fabrication of the truth was problematic and disturbing to those of us who knew what was really happening. But we also believed, naively, that Reagan's administration would end with the completion of his first term and with his departure that the war back home would end too.

The irony of it all is significant looking back on things. It is striking that so many of us Salvadoran refugees are still here in the United States, living and working in this country. Almost all of us assumed a return to our homeland at some not-too-distant point in time. The idea of returning to a newly reformed society gave us the incentive to accelerate our work, even when things got very tough for us here and in El Salvador, because we wanted to bring the Reagan policies to an end and we wanted to inspire a robust democratic change in our own country. Sadly, all of that turned out different than we hoped. It was completely out of our hands. So we stayed on and created a new life for ourselves here, but one that remained very connected in important ways to where we came from.

Upon making our way from Washington to Los Angeles, my wife and I found a surprising degree of Salvadoran community activism and support there. In Los Angeles I took up work with a group of other political refugees, although we were not acknowledged as such in those days. Amongst ourselves, however, we were already self-defining as refugees, by that time, because that is what we were. We came from a war, from a persecution, and we were fleeing that. I started assisting a refugee committee called Santa Chirino Amaya, which was already established; it was not just beginning as most U.S.-based

Salvadoran organizations were back then. It had already taken some first, important steps to advance our movement by supporting our emerging community of exiles in the United States. It had established a clinic that provided free medical services to the community and it also had developed a public advocacy organization called El Rescate (the Rescue) that provided social and legal immigration aid to Salvadoran refugees, as well as many Guatemalans who had started arriving in large numbers to Los Angeles for their own political reasons.

After a short while, I worked as the receptionist at El Rescate because my colleagues thought I was the best English-speaker within our leadership group. For this reason, they suspected that I might do a better job than anyone else fielding calls from mainstream policy, media and funding leaders. That work proved to be too passive for me, though. I quickly found myself engaged in more activist work in the organization's social services department, but with a strong emphasis on community organizing. In fact, organizing was our main goal. We wanted to help our service and community clients become more informed of the issues taking shape in response to the El Salvador war and we wanted to engage them in addressing those issues through direct involvement in the Solidarity Movement. So the provision of social services is what enabled us initially to get people working with our activist refugee committee. Refugees would come to El Rescate looking for legal aid and social help, and we would work with them in those areas while also activating them to support solidarity activities.

After the passage of more time, I went to work as a director of social services, then as director of a hostel for Central American refugees. From there I became active on a range of other refugee community projects, each time with more responsibility and public exposure. A lot of these activities involved me in planning and overseeing important initiatives and events. I remember, for example, that as we started to develop the Solidarity Movement, we became more strategic and formal in our collaborations with U.S. activists, most of them adherents of various religious faiths. We grew together through these collaborations and my role was to help facilitate this work. We would plant the seeds of direction based on what we felt was needed and our North American partners would nurture them. In time, our work evolved to become more aggressive. People started during this time to take material goods down to El Salvador and also to mobilize around stronger direct support to the U.S.-based refugees, but not in their luggage anymore; instead, they started to provide this support in bulk quantities. They organized excursions that were in effect political, exploratory trips to El Salvador to see what was taking place there; and in conjunction with those trips our North American allies brought the Salvadoran people items that they desperately needed, from food to medicine. I helped to organize this sort of exchange activity. We worked a lot, enough to create caravans with many vehicles and people to take goods to El Salvador.

Along the way, some of our work benefited from unanticipated developments. A good example of this was the devastating earthquake that shook El Salvador during 1986. It mobilized people because the nation had been badly hit by this catastrophe. After the persecution and the bombing that had rocked El Salvador in preceding years, the earthquake damaged many thousands of homes and many people were left without shelter and basic services. We took advantage of this situation to help more and we started an organization called Building with the Voiceless of El Salvador, primarily with the help of committed North Americans and a few Salvadorans, like myself, who worked with them. In addition to providing direct aid to earthquake victims, Building with the Voiceless did solidarity and political work. We lobbied the U.S. Congress, took direct action in El Salvador and Honduras, organized refugee camps, and secured new funding for emerging anchor organizations in the movement like El Rescate and our community clinic. A lot of good work was accomplished in this way.

Looking back on things it is important to acknowledge that there was not just one center of gravity in this work. It was more complicated than that. In the final analysis, our efforts were related to but importantly distinct from those of the emerging Sanctuary Movement. I see our work in the Solidarity Movement as having been rooted in a certain direct political activism focused on change within El Salvador. The Sanctuary Movement, on the other hand, was in the end a purely religious movement focused mainly on U.S. political dynamics. Presbyterians had much to do with the beginning of that movement, and they turned it into a national movement that was opposed politically to the politics of Ronald Reagan in Central America, especially El

Salvador. They did everything—hunger strikes, acts of civil disobedience and community organizing, to the degree that they would go to the places where their supporters were to train them on how to protest peacefully. In the end, they organized protests that had great impact in the United States at both the local and the national levels.

Together, these two tracks of activity—Solidarity and Sanctuary—established a powerful combination of resistance that ultimately had a large impact on changing U.S. and Salvadoran government antidemocratic policy. Ultimately, I think that I helped both sets of efforts by participating in them at various times and in various ways. I did what I could for both movements with the skills I had to offer. I educated people and spoke with them on the issues: Salvadorans, Guatemalans and North Americans. Throughout much of this period, I had the opportunity to travel across the United States to speak about the situation in our country and our refugee community's need for funds and other support to resist what was happening there. I also traveled on numerous occasions to Central America with North Americans who wanted to see the situation firsthand.

Like so many of us, I did most of what I did without meaningful financial compensation. Many of us, in fact, did this work for almost nothing; this is a reality that we cannot deny. But we really wanted to work for change and we believed in what we were doing. I worked in the organizations refugees themselves formed in Los Angeles and other parts of the United States without a salary or stipend for several years. It was not until later, thanks largely to the efforts of my family here (and especially my mother) that I was able to find regular, paid work to sustain me. But even with the lack of pay and other support, I think that my early and sustained participation in numerous meetings, discussions and arrangements positively affected things that happened during that time in the community and political realms. I gave sixteen years of my life to activism and endless running to advance this work. Now I see it all as only one rushed breath of time. In my perception it is as if those sixteen years, because of their relentless demands and constant pressures, were compressed into one.

I think that is the essence of civic and democratic participation. One does all that is humanly possible to achieve changes in public governance that enable people to achieve their highest potential. I guess in the future, where the work we did is concerned, experts can analyze whether we were truly effective; but, from a humanitarian and political point of view, I believe we did a lot, we achieved a lot. Important groups and networks were formed. People spoke out and protested at a political level who had never done so before. People learned to engage their public representatives, their elected officials on the issues. They were many times successful in encouraging those officials to change their beliefs where they had been against us initially and to shift their votes and prestige in support of our movement in Congress and other key decision-making venues. Our efforts also helped people who we involved in this work learn how to influence foreign aid for El Salvador and other countries—that was another achievement of our generation. In these many ways, I think that what we did was effective and important.

In addition to the aforementioned impacts of our work, we also advanced very practical activities that made a positive contribution to our community and civil society. For example, our impacts on human rights advocacy and law were substantial. By raising international awareness of human rights violations in El Salvador and the gross complexities of how they happened, we did a lot to accelerate justice and government reforms across Latin America. Our efforts made clear that official injustices in places like El Salvador were not simply a matter of assassinating a few targeted leaders, but also of removing everyday people from their living quarters, restraining them without formal charges in military control zones and denying them basic needs to live or survive, disappearing people without notice of who had been detained and without putting them through a trial or even accusing them of anything concrete. Our efforts revealed that, contrary to constitutional requirements in our nation, people were simply being detained, tortured and killed on entirely unsubstantiated government and vigilante group suspicions that they were terrorists or subversives. All of these practices constituted clear human rights violations.

Through groups like El Rescate, we started to look into this because people all over Central and Latin America started to tell us of such things happening in their countries too. And we started working on the idea of organizing an exhaustive investigation of human rights violations across the Central American region and the Southern Cone, in countries like Brazil, Argentina and Chile. We sent an international delegation to conduct an investigation. The result became a United Nations-supported study that documented the many violations we uncovered, including who was responsible and affected in each case, what exactly was transpiring in each context, how many people were victimized, etc. We also advanced a set of proposals for bringing the violating nations and their leaders to justice. Through this work, we set in motion international criminal justice efforts that continue to matter still today. An example of this is in Chile, where the former dictator, General Augusto Pinochet, continues to be prosecuted even after his death in 2006. International law rulings handed Pinochet back over to Chilean authorities to face justice for his crimes against humanity in that country, which he and his government committed more than thirty years ago.

Our efforts ultimately helped to educate and involve many common, committed people in areas and ways that enabled them to become more fully a part of democratic society. We mobilized a lot of people to help us document and publicize lists of individuals whose rights had been violated. We engaged people in efforts to identify the victims who had been assassinated or bombed, or disappeared. In fact, here in Los Angeles, we built an enormous wall in a park on which we posted thousands of names of the disappeared and the assassinated. We featured the victims' real names, which were provided to us by their surviving relatives. It is very similar to the monument for the fallen of the Vietnam War that sits in Washington, DC. The concept of our memorial wall in Los Angeles was ultimately replicated in El Salvador: Indeed, in El Cuzcatlán Park in San Salvador there is now a wall that also names the many who died during the war of the 1980s.

In addition to these many important aspects of our work and legacy dating back to the war, our efforts back then played a key role in bringing about the peace accords that ultimately ended the worst of the madness in El Salvador and the other nations of Central America. Indeed, our work, particularly in the international law field, defined the basic negotiating framework that resulted in these peace treaties. While there have been continuing issues in El Salvador and within the region since, to be sure, our efforts provided a solid foundation to support the end of the worst conditions and practices that had prevailed in the predating period of Central American history.

The end of the war, however, did not mark the end of our movement. In the years since, groups like El Rescate have continued to play a significant role in helping to advance the rights and opportunities of Salvadorans who have remained in large numbers in the United States, as well as those who have continued to reside in El Salvador in the post-war period. After developing strong social services programs and legal advocacy efforts related to Salvadoran immigration status concerns and the like, we developed and pursued important economic development programs designed to create employment and income-generating opportunities for our transnational community. In this work, we started with a group of Central American youths, to train them in office work or as possible future community leaders and organizers. The most promising graduates of this program then came to work at El Rescate. They worked with the more experienced members of our staff, both North American and Salvadoran, who had been central to solidarity and who transmitted much of their experience to the youth so that they might later advance similar leadership.

A large part of this work was U.S.-focused, because it became clear even after the war's end that a majority of the Salvadoran refugee community that was in the United States by that point was not going back to El Salvador. That group of people had already settled into U.S. life, it had invested in this country and it was simply not going to return to our nation of origin. One of the practical realities of this situation was the need to ground our community in greater knowledge about the requirements and ways of the U.S. economy. We needed to prepare our people to survive and thrive in the United States from an economic and asset management point of view. Recognizing this reality, within our department of economic development at El Rescate, we began then to consider creating a savings and credit cooperative.

I participated in the early investigations giving rise to the later formation of El Rescate's savings and credit cooperative. For practical reasons, the idea quickly evolved into a collaboration with Santana Chirino Amaya, which helped us to organize Salvadorans in specific towns both in the United States and in El Salvador. In each place where we became active, people from participating communities on either the U.S side or the Salvadoran side, took up together a series of activities to raise funds for community-building projects in El Salvador. Through these efforts, U.S.-based Salvadorans would amass resources and send them to their home towns to support specific, mutually agreed projects. Projects would thus be supported to improve streets in certain localities, to provide better schools, to renovate local churches, to fix the mayor's office and comparable things of this sort.

This model of international cooperation and joint investment—which actually dated back to the very incipiency of our movement—was ultimately implemented in large scale more than a decade later during the 1990s, in various regions of El Salvador—fourteen altogether. From the beginning, the idea was to make this something for the people, on an individual or family level. But in time we realized that we could also do good through this work at the community-wide level. And that is how we formed the Cooperativa de Ahorro y Crédito Comunidades (Communities Credit and Savings Cooperative) that in the beginning was to be called Comunidades de Ayuda Directa a El Salvador (Direct Assistance Communities for El Salvador).

The latter was the name of the movement we envisioned to raise funds for the towns in El Salvador that had suffered most as a result of the repression and war of the 1980s. The work we began at that time (we actually started this work as early as 1977) is still ongoing, it is still functioning as a working cooperative, providing banking services to community members who do not otherwise have access to them. The cooperative provides loans to people who do not have access to the formal banking system because of a lack of credit history. It also facilitates remittance payments of earned wages and savings by Salvadoran residents of this nation to their needy relatives in El Salvador.

These transactions in turn have helped many families and communities in El Salvador to sustain themselves in the years since the war and violence ended. They have enabled Salvadoran gardeners and building contractors, for example, to purchase heavy vehicles in which to transport their tools and machinery. They have also helped lower-middle income white-collar families to buy a family car that is not new but that allows them to move more comfortably from their homes to their work and vice versa. These are important gains that our work has helped the people of El Salvador to achieve.

Our work in this area was distinguished early on by virtue of being more than a money-lending and profit-making proposition. We consciously organized this work around a cooperative model, rather than a traditional banking model. Our interest was in building strong, democratic communities in post-war El Salvador. So the financial institution we established goes well beyond simply lending. It promotes community capital formation and investment through special, incentive-based savings programs. It sponsors a special program for youth who have completed the ninth grade, donating a dollar for every dollar those young people save so that when they graduate high school they have amassed $3,000 to help them to attain a college degree or a professional training credential.

Our work in these areas reflects the important difference between a credit bank, which merely supports financial transactions, and a cooperative, which is really more about collective community building. Today, there are still some 1,500 registered members of the cooperative we started. People are really getting to know about this work more than anywhere else in the Pico-Union district of downtown Los Angeles, where one of the most concentrated populations of U.S. Salvadorans and Central Americans live. But, of course, the people who benefit from this work are not only the ones who live in Los Angeles; there are many beneficiaries who participate in this work all across the hemisphere.

Summing up, I think that the work done in the United States by refugees like myself put El Salvador on the map. That is, at least from a U.S. and developed nation standpoint, El Salvador was a largely unknown country through the 1970s; but, if you look at it now, most informed North American and world leaders now know something about El Salvador, as do most average people in important political centers. And increasingly, I believe, here in the United States, Salvadorans are recognized as a group of people who came here not necessarily to absorb or extract resources from this country, but on the contrary to create new resources. For example, quickly after its formation El Rescate became a significant source of new employment for many people. It was a nonprofit organization that managed to raise more than two million dollars annually for its budget. And we paid taxes on those two million dollars. Our work thus created an important economic engine within and from our communities that enabled people to live legally in the United States and to become a part of the national workforce. To this day, Salvadoran Americans, like other foreign-born residents of the United States, continue to provide important economic benefits to this country.

Our experience in the United States has also produced important human relations and policy contributions that benefit our people and U.S. interests as well. During the early years of our movement for solidarity and sanctuary, for example, our people traveled throughout the United States and created goodwill everywhere they went. Our early, close work with important religious leaders and communities was especially ground-breaking in relation to expanding tolerance and cross-cultural understanding in many U.S. communities, both large and small. In addition to these many contributions to American civic culture, refugees from El Salvador laid the groundwork for important changes in U.S. immigration and humanitarian policy that afforded temporary protected status for selected groups of political refugees. On this basis, with good cause, qualifying refugees may now be granted temporary asylum in the United States for up to eighteen months. This special status allows protected individuals to work and move throughout the United States without restrictions, so long as they remain law-abiding, tax-paying members of U.S. society. Honduran, Guatemalan refugees and others have also benefited in recent years from these protective arrangements—arrangements that extend the United States moral strength and standing to promote democratic practices internationally.

Finally, in more recent years, as our communities have become more grounded in long-standing U.S. traditions, we have also helped to embolden American democracy through our increasingly robust involvement in U.S. electoral politics. You can see this in our recent contributions to the election of new political leaders, like our new mayor here in Los Angeles, Antonio Villaraigosa. Because of our substantial support for the new mayor's candidacy, Salvadorans have become an important part of the work that Villaraigosa does in relation to policy formation and outreach. And more and more Salvadorans or people of Salvadoran origin are becoming part of an elite of elected and appointed officials in this country, in California and elsewhere. I am talking about people like California state senator Liz Figueroa. Through the work of these leaders, Salvadorans have begun to influence political and social thought in Washington and other important places; and in the process they are laying the groundwork for a new politics in other countries, like El Salvador.

My reflections on all of these contributions give me a sense of satisfaction and accomplishment, even though it has been seven years since I left El Rescate and the Solidarity Movement. I have continued with social work in the sense that I have been working closely with Latino families that have small children—newborns to age five—helping them with advice on how to raise their kids in a healthy emotional and mental environment. I also have been working in recent years with homeless women who are ready to stop being indigent by learning responsibility, securing work and a place to live, paying their own rent, etc. I try to help them take the necessary steps to move into safe, clean, inexpensive dwellings and to establish and maintain the discipline needed to live productively in society. I help them access education and training programs that prepare them not only to find work but also to keep it, because losing employment is usually the presenting problem that created their homelessness to begin with.

As I think ahead to the future of the Salvadoran community in the United States, I see us slowly but surely becoming more a part of the establishment. I am referring to the fact that we see more and more Salvadorans succeeding in various key fields: politics, business and academia come to mind. This is good. But I also worry sometimes that we may be losing focus on the transnational origins of our population. Most of our emerging leaders in this nation, even those who were born in El Salvador, increasingly tend to focus their efforts on U.S.-based concerns. There are good reasons for this given our community's many still-pressing needs for opportunity and equality in America, particularly given the growing anti-immigrant policy sentiment we see emerging in many parts of the nation.

But I really do not see these politics as being sufficient. I believe we need in the future to confront issues beyond the essentially internal concerns of the United States. We need to recognize that we live in and are affected by global realities and that North Americans have special capacities and reasons to act more responsibly in this context. We have to recognize that we have important stakes in other parts of the world that should be informing our policies in different directions.

For example, even despite the huge Salvadoran population that now exists in California (more than one million people), California still does not meaningfully concern itself with what happens in El Salvador from a political or economic standpoint. It should. There are important continuing issues that deserve more joint attention from political leaders both in the United States and El Salvador. But I do not see as much recognition of this reality as I would like. Hopefully in the years to come this will change. But, for the time being, it seems as if the Solidarity Movement has diminished to relative inactivity. The war ended, the alleged persecution, but there are still serious problems that require active leadership attention, problems related to economic development, health, education and other needs.

These lingering problems in El Salvador could give rise at any time to another serious situation there; but there are precious few Salvadorans or others these days working to prevent, stop or even warn of an impending crisis. Sometimes, I look at the Salvadoran community and see that we are so focused now on becoming part of the so-called American melting pot that we have lost sight of the unique experiences and responsibilities that brought us here where our own nation and people are concerned. I see a growing apathy in us in this connection.

During the 1980s and 1990s, important political and economic information on El Salvador and the United States flowed freely. Now, although we have the Internet and we can communicate almost instantaneously with one another, there is not much information available on El Salvador or its relationship with the United States that is meaningful and politically significant. One does hear, sporadically, about growing social problems in El Salvador, such as the growing phenomenon of U.S.-style gangs, and how they are killing each other. There is likewise talk about increasing sexual violations of children in El Salvador and the like; but one does not hear about the still problematic economic and political situation in El Salvador and throughout the Americas that gives rise to these growing challenges, unless there is a national election or a major event.

Increasingly, it seems, the refugee generation from El Salvador is settling here in the United States, and one finds it thus being more concerned with surviving or living comfortably in American society than remaining connected to El Salvador, Latin America and the past. That is, here we mainly think about material considerations—that we must have money to live well, that we must have money to dress well, to eat well, to study well, to travel well and to do all that. But the conditions that created the El Salvador war of the 1980s and the related flight of refugees seeking freedom still prevail in important respects in that nation: lack of meaningful political rights, oppressive employment conditions and pay and inadequate support systems for the needy and those who through their hard work contribute most to Salvadoran society.

I think that what is happening is that the monster is sleeping. I think it will wake up one day again and that we will need to reorient our focus back to basics. A new discussion or debate has to begin, a new way of thinking about addressing the evolving problems that El Salvador is facing. I do not think this next phase of challenge will necessarily be like the political era that brought most of us Salvadorans to the United States in the 1980s. We surely will face something more distinctive than that; but our challenges will nevertheless involve activating organized networks of action to advance the innovations and changes required to benefit the people.

I see myself still being active in that next phase movement, participating in the debate of what our organizational strategy should be, what change models we should support in the United States and in El Salvador, etc. I also see myself as one who could serve again as a bridge-builder between the U.S.-based Salvadoran refugee community and the Salvadoran citizenry that has remained in El Salvador. We are united, whether we like it or not, even if it is true that a vast distance separates us. Our people here, even now, continue working endless hours at multiple jobs at a time to care for and support their families over there. And people over there still think of us as their sons and daughters, their cousins and extended family members.

Our experiences during the 1980s offer important lessons for the future. I think that we must acknowledge, for example, that none of the work advanced then was done individually. All the experiences lived, all the results, all that is left there is part of an enormous legacy of collective work. We must also never forget those who sacrificed the most, those who gave their lives. For example, there was a group of twelve Salvadorans who died during the height of the asylum struggle, asphyxiated in a van on the Arizona desert, trying desperately to come to the United States in search of freedom. Their deaths laid the groundwork for the important work of the Sanctuary Movement in the United States. We have to remember that those of us who survived are responsible to tell the stories of those who did not make it. I would like to state clearly that I am only a grain of sand in this immensity that has been the Solidarity Movement in the United States. It is with others that our efforts can sum to something that is ultimately bigger and more effective than any of us alone can ever be.

One of the reasons why my grandfather is still part of my life is because when I think of the history of El Salvador, I think of him. He was the first person to tell me about the history of El Salvador. He told me about it because he was immersed in the situation that ultimately gave rise to the horrors of the 1980s. During my youth, I would often read him historical recounts of the incidents he told me of and point up differences in the books' or articles' reporting. He would tell me emphatically: "No, the situation was not like they say there. It happened differently." He remembered exact events with dates and times, and that was impressive to me. As things turned out, my grandfather told me the history of El Salvador and its people and, later, I lived it. Everything that he told me, I experienced it. We would dig holes; my siblings and I dug to find our dead brother. My grandfather dug holes in his youth too, to bury Indians killed as a part of the government genocide of his era; the government forced him to do so.

Recounting this history is what inspires me to insist that we have to start thinking of what we are going to do the next time there is a crisis in El Salvador, because I am convinced, as my grandfather was, that history is preparing to repeat itself there with each passing year. I think that, in the years ahead, we cannot allow ourselves to let El Salvador merely repeat the same punishing and counter-productive history over and over again. We have to break this vicious circle in which the story repeats itself with only slight changes in vocabulary, characteristics and ideological influences. I do not want my grandchildren to have to tell their grandchildren of their participation in a Salvadoran Solidarity Movement in the United States as they prepare a book. I want them to tell their grandchildren that El Salvador, with the work of their grandparents, was able to achieve great democratic and economic gains that broke the cycle of an earlier repetitive history of killing and inequality. Hopefully, this will be our legacy.

Alicia Mendoza

My earliest memories take me back to an event that took place on September 7, 1944, in the place where I was born—Santiago de María, El Salvador. On that date, a pilgrimage of Catholics left for Puerto de la Unión. A man from Santiago de María who had been living in Puerto de la Unión, when he heard that there was a pilgrimage planned from the town he was from, he invited everyone to go for a boat ride. There are no rivers, ponds or anything like that to speak of in Santiago de María; so people from the town were very excited to accept the man's invitation. They boarded his boat at a small port location some miles away where it was docked. They came in large numbers and in good humor; I think there were about eighty people in the pilgrimage.

Once the boat was a couple of miles from shore, many people moved to one side of it, and it capsized. About seventy people drowned. It was terrible. I remember that I was at school. When I heard the news, which was broadcast on the speakers at the local movie theater, there was hysteria. People ran all over the place. The horrible event had a particularly strong impact on me because seven members of my family died. Many children and young people were among the ones who drowned. The elder women survived because the longer, more old-fashioned skirts they were wearing allowed them to remain afloat. When they recovered the bodies of those who drowned, they laid them out on the shoreline to be reclaimed by their families and loved ones. I have never forgotten that.

Another event that I vividly recall occurred that same year, in 1944. I remember that is when I began to hear about political parties. Back then, Martínez was in power and there was an opposition candidate by the name of Dr. Romero, who was loved by many people. During the evenings, campaign workers would go house-by-house inviting people to political meetings and rallies that were to be held at various locations in town. I remember one night there was an event that scared me a lot—a protest at about six in the evening. The protest ended with a lot of loud fights and violence.

I used to live with my grandmother, and that evening, owing to the unrest around town, we must have ended up with about twenty people hiding in the bathroom of our house. Outside, we heard gunshots, screams and people running from one side of the street to the other trying to avoid being apprehended and killed. It was a very long night; the madness lasted about six or seven hours. On the following day, when we were able to go outside, it was overwhelming to hear about and see everything that had taken place. As we went around our town, we saw near total destruction. Houses had been burned, people were incarcerated, were dead or missing. That is another experience that powerfully impacted me during my childhood.

I left El Salvador on December 10, 1959, the same way that many people did in those days and continue to do now—as a poor young person in search of opportunity. I come from a large family of seven brothers and sisters. My mother was a breadmaker and my father was a tailor. We lived in extreme poverty. I had to leave San Salvador at age fourteen to learn to sew, so that I could make a living. But I quickly realized that I was not a good seamstress. In time, I started working in a pharmacy as a salesperson and filling out prescriptions. However hard I worked, though, I could make only about 30 *colones* every month. During that time, food was very cheap, but I was just not making enough money to survive. That is why I seized the opportunity to come to the United States when it was presented to me in 1959.

I had been living entirely on my own in San Salvador, except for one friend I made in the hostel in which I lived. It was run by charity nuns and they had a house called El amparo de las jóvenes, or the Shelter for Young Women. Living there were many other young girls who, like me, had come to the capitol either to study or to work or both. During that time, I met a girl who had a friend with relatives in Florida and they told her of a family who needed a girl from El Salvador to come and work with them in Miami to baby-sit. My friend did not want to go and she said, "Licha, do you want to go the United States?" (People called me 'Licha' then.)

I answered, "Yes, I'll go to the United States, but what will I do?"

"Take care of children, work with a family," my friend replied.

"Oh, yes, I'll go," I said. I knew that I was being offered a once in a lifetime opportunity, and I took advantage of it and left El Salvador to baby-sit in the United States.

I arrived in Miami and the family took me in. They were Latinos: The woman was Salvadoran and the man was from Puerto Rico. I had to take care of their four children. At first, it all seemed like a dream come true; but I quickly learned about disillusionment at the hands of the very family that I thought would be my saviors and protectors. In the beginning, like most young people, I had many illusions about the hard realities of life. I thought that once I settled in the United States, my dream would be completed. But I did not know then all that awaited me. The lady whom I came to work for in Florida told me immediately upon my arrival that she intended to discount from my first several pay checks all the money she had spent to bring me on—my air fare, legal paper work, etc.—and that she would only be paying me $30 per month, substantially less than I had been promised during our negotiations before I came to the United States. From those $30, I had to send $20 each month to my mother back in El Salvador in order to help my family. It was very frustrating for me, but I would tell myself that it was all part of the sacrifice I had to endure for the opportunity to come to North America. In fact, my Miami employers knew well that once I had arrived at their doorstep there was little, indeed nothing I could do to defend myself in a compensation struggle, short of returning to my country.

In the end, I had to put up with their many abuses precisely because I did *not* want to return to El Salvador. I knew somehow that my chances for success in life were deeply connected with the opportunity to live and work in North America. But I told myself that I was not going back to El Salvador because my work in Miami was the opportunity that would allow my other siblings to go to school. This was an important consideration and motivation, since I had not been lucky enough to get an education. I only attended elementary school because my family could not afford anything else and also because I did not have the basic skills to succeed in a more advanced curriculum owing to the disadvantages presented by El Salvador's poverty.

Back then, there was no basic plan, remedial program or anything like that available to keep me or others like me in school.

The experience in Miami tested me at every turn. I suffered a lot working for that family. They mistreated me, handling me as rich people treated the poor back in Latin America. They never physically abused me, but they would abuse me in other ways and I often felt quite humiliated. At the same time, I knew that what I was going through in those moments would not be forever. I knew that my life was going to change one day. What ultimately justified my patience was that the dreaded Miami family for which I worked initially had pre-arranged my official status to enable me to travel to, remain and work in the U.S. legally. That is how I became a permanent resident of the United States; I did not enter illegitimately. This was a great advantage for me, though initially, out of ignorance, I really did not fully understand its significance. As it turned out, in time it became evident to me that my legal status in the United States afforded me certain rights and privileges, choices and powers that I had never known before. I came to appreciate these prerogatives more fully when out of frustration, I fled the Miami household to seek employment elsewhere. My act of defiance produced a lot of stress for me, raising lots of issues about loyalty and so on. But my desire to flee was so strong that I simply had to leave.

I looked for employment in a newspaper and soon went to work at a home where I baby-sat two children. There I was paid only $20 per week, but I felt relieved enough about not being in my former circumstances that I felt better. Because I ran away from the first family for which I had worked in Miami, I was always afraid during this period that the police would arrest me and that I might be deported. I was not aware of my rights. But, strikingly, when I finally received my resident alien card, the family that had initially brought me to the United States and from which I had run did not take it from me. I later learned this was because they could not legally do so. Fearing the worst if I were detected in my new employment situation, I called the Salvadoran consul in Miami. He asked me to come see him and I did. At our meeting, he told me not to fear anything since I was in the United States legally. He assured me that I could work anywhere I chose and he told me that I did not have to hide. I also found out that he knew my family. After my visit with the consul, I felt safe.

Soon thereafter, I was told that a wealthy Cuban family was looking for a babysitter. So I went and interviewed for the job at the family's home. It was a luxurious mansion in Miami. The owners were followers of Batista, who had fled during the weeks following Castro's overthrow of the Bautista regime. They treated me really well and the salary they offered me was a whopping $40 a week.

In the beginning, my work for the Cuban family was difficult because the two children that I had to look after treated me quite badly. They were rude and disrespectful. But, little by little, I got them to like me and, in time, they ended up loving me. I also gained their parents' trust. After only a few short months, they told me I no longer had to eat in the kitchen; instead, I was invited to dine with them.

I remember that they gave me money to go back to El Salvador on a vacation. I went to visit my family after two years. I took many things for my family and I stayed there two months. I returned to Miami and to my position with the Cuban family, but I soon learned that they did not want to say in Miami and they left for Europe, to Spain. In fact, during the time that I had been working for them, the Cuban family traveled several times to Spain and took me with them. Each time, we traveled on a luxurious boat. It was beautiful. I had never imagined that I would ever travel on a boat like that. I would think of when I was a child harvesting coffee on the plantation; and then I saw myself where I was at that moment. I really could not believe where life had taken me. On one trip, I spent two months in Spain with the Cuban family. I saw many places and traveled throughout Spain. It was as if I had become a part of the family. In time, they stopped treating me like a babysitter altogether.

One day, the woman of the house told me that she and her husband and children wanted me to move to Spain with them. I was honored, but also intimidated. I felt that living in Spain would take me even further away from El Salvador and my family. The thought frightened me. Moving to Spain was not what I wanted to do. So I declined the family's generous offer. In time, I decided to move to California with a couple of girlfriends from Guatemala and El Salvador whom I had met in Miami. We were all looking for a change and so much seemed to be happening in San Francisco. When we arrived on the West Coast, we immediately had to get work to survive. My first job was in a rest home taking care of the elderly. After that, I worked in hotels, factories and kitchens—a bunch of places like that; whatever it took to pay the bills. Little by little, I met people and made a life for myself in the Bay Area.

Along the way, I had a baby and when she was little I started working as a teacher's aide at my daughter's pre-school. I worked at the school for about four years, and I saw my daughter grow up there until she went to kindergarten. After that I enrolled in a cosmetology school, but when I completed my school and went to cut hair I could not keep a job because of the work hours; I had to work on Sundays and I did not have anyone to take care of my daughter. So, after awhile, I concluded that working as a hair stylist was not for me after all. From then on, I started looking for another type of work. By that time, my daughter was getting to be about ten years old and the Sanctuary and Solidarity Movements were developing. I quickly became heavily involved in this work and gained the friendship and support of the many people with whom I collaborated on various committees.

I knew that I could no longer come from work to my house and watch television or *telenovelas*. I was now involved in something much bigger than that, where I could be highly useful and help people I knew in El Salvador. That is when I realized that although I did not have an education at a university level, I could contribute quite a bit. I am very satisfied that my contribution has been well-recognized, and I feel good about the fact that still today, because if what I did then, I am recognized by political activists and others almost everywhere I go.

In the course of the war, there were many family separations created by political differences. Some in my family for example, quickly took to calling me and my colleagues communists, and that deeply divided us. But in time, with the war's conclusion, we recovered and that all stayed in the past. When I went to El Salvador last time, it had been about twenty-five years since I had communicated with certain members of my family because of our divergent political views. I went to look for them and they graciously saw me. They heard of more recent community-building work that I had been doing for El Salvador and they congratulated me.

These sorts of experiences reveal what is important in life and that is why recounting them in publications like this one is essential. I always thought that I could provide a testimony like the one I am giving today because doing so would allow many people to read it and become aware of the long-term affect of the war in El Salvador. It is vital that everyone knows who participated in the conflict and in what ways. Therefore, this is a story that we had to write. It is a very rich story with continuing lessons, and I believe that this book will help many generations, especially the children, to better understand what it was all about.

Even here in the United States there are many Salvadoran families and many children in those families who do not know that there was a war, they do not know what happened. They do not know their own history. I believe that it is a beautiful thing that in the future those children will be able to read all of my thoughts here and those of other activists who played important roles in the struggle. Several years ago a Salvadoran poet told me he wanted to write my story. Unfortunately all of our tape-recorded interviews were later lost. It is a great shame because it would have been nice to have someone write my story. But since that could not happen, I am pleased to share some of the key aspects of that story here with you.

After becoming very active in El Salvador-related political activities in California, I became fairly known around the San Francisco Bay Area for my leadership on behalf of the cause. But it was not always like that. Initially, I came to this work somewhat by accident and as something of a political novice. One of the first events in which I participated was a demonstration that a small group of Salvadorans organized. I think it was in August of 1976. We mounted a protest concerning the university student massacre that had just then occurred in El Salvador. The massacre took place because the students had aggressively protested the government's sponsorship of the Miss Universe pageant, while it denied salary and wage increases to university faculty and diminished funding for state-supported university scholarships.

The Salvadoran government's outrageous response in massacring the students compelled us, a group of about twenty to twenty-five Salvadorans living in San Francisco, to mobilize a small march. The march was intended to raise North Americans' awareness of the atrocities beginning to emerge at this time in our country. From then on, my community participation and political activism grew. I became more involved in progressive political activities, especially related to El Salvador, and we started to organize ourselves to do whatever we could to challenge the government's increasingly repressive policies.

During this period, I had the opportunity to meet many Chilean exiles living in San Francisco. They had all been banished from their country by the Pinochet regime, which had begun to disappear political dissidents. We would meet at my house and they would play the guitar. I started to learn more about the political situation in other parts of Latin America, what all those Chileans had gone through. After that, the Sandinista Revolution took place in Nicaragua and I became politically involved in supporting that effort. Many Salvadoran Americans began to march with Nicaraguans on the streets around this time and it was very impressive to me, to see thousands and thousands of people marching on the streets of San Francisco. I used to like to walk the protest route with a large megaphone. I was the one who would yell the slogans, because people would say that my voice was strong and I was thus always strategically placed at the forefront of our major marches. That is how the years passed during my early chapters in California.

The Sandinista electoral triumph in Nicaragua came in 1979 and we continued in our work, focusing now increasingly on the war in El Salvador. There was a lot going on in El Salvador during these years. We had so many groups and events to raise funds for, to support the Solidarity Movement that was then emerging. We made tamales to sell and organized afternoon parties and other events. We participated in all the marches and demonstrations that were taking place in and around San Francisco. There was truly no El Salvador-related event that we did not go out for during this time, to protest and raise funds.

During the early stages of our work on El Salvador, a comrade and I came up with the idea of supporting music festivals to raise funds and awareness in support of our cause. It made great sense to us because our entire generation had gotten its progressive political inspiration largely from popular songs. In 1981, we launched the first musical festival for El Salvador in Berkeley. Nine hundred people came out for the event and it was really nice because many community-based solidarity groups participated. It was a beautiful gathering; that concert inspired people. From that moment on, I felt that the way I could contribute best to the movement was through music, and I got deeply involved in organizing other concerts and music festivals. I experienced the power of music again in 1984, when I had the opportunity to participate in a leadership gathering of Central American activists in Ecuador as a representative for Salvadoran women. The gathering was accompanied by a festival of protest songs that lasted two weeks. There, I had the opportunity to meet and bond with many activist leaders from across the western hemisphere and Europe. I still keep in touch with many of them.

My engagements in connection with El Salvador were multiple. I participated heavily in both the Sanctuary and Solidarity Movements. In San Francisco, the first movement that really took hold was Sanctuary, because many Salvadoran refugees started coming from El Salvador relatively early in the conflict. My friends in the struggle and I often gathered at churches and participated in hunger strikes. In the Bay Area, the first sanctuary efforts that took place were in Berkeley and then in San Francisco. In both places, we created safe heavens for Salvadoran refugees who had to be protected from being returned to El Salvador because most were undocumented. Many of these people were political enemies of the Salvadoran government and death squads, but the U.S. government failed in most cases to recognize them as political refugees. As a result, the only thing that stood between these progressive political figures and certain torture, even death back in El Salvador was our sanctuary support.

As political progress evolved more slowly to forge needed democratic reforms in El Salvador, I also became involved in the Solidarity Movement; but that came a little later. My main early focus was on sanctuary. Important religious leaders also followed this pattern of engagement. The Lutheran and Catholic churches, for example, started to get involved in sanctuary and sanctuaries began to open within the churches themselves, to provide housing to the many refugees who were arriving in the United States. As circumstances worsened, the people of El Salvador, especially those most persecuted by the government and its allies, began to take more extreme measures to leave the country. At one point, several Salvadorans died as they were crossing the Arizona desert on a caravan in search of international humanitarian protection. A survivor of that horrible experience is still with us. His name is José Cartagena and he survived what happened in the desert. That story had a large impact everywhere. It highlighted the extent of desperation circulating among the Salvadoran populace as a result of the brutal dictatorship that ruled the land with U.S. government backing. We organized a huge campaign around those issues and that is when the Catholic and Lutheran churches really started to get more involved and to provide asylum to those displaced by the war.

As events unfolded, I deepened my involvement in efforts to use music concerts as a vehicle for generating new funds and interest on behalf of political reform in El Salvador, here in the United States. When I went to Ecuador I was able to establish contacts with many talented and committed musicians, with many bands from the United States and other countries. After I returned from that gathering, I started calling all those people and I asked them if they wanted to participate in a benefit concert for El Salvador in San Francisco. They remembered me perfectly well and many people accepted my invitation. Through my efforts, we were also able to book a group of African American women who live in Washington, D.C. and perform without instruments. They are known as Sweet Honey in the Rock. They are very famous, and they came to San Francisco twice to perform on our behalf. They produced beautiful and very well-attended concerts. I then organized another large event with Jackson Brown, the rock-n-roll hall of fame legend, who was just then becoming a very strong activist in the movement. Initially, I did not know who he was, but he accepted my invitation enthusiastically and eventually came to San Francisco several times to perform and raise funds for the people of El Salvador.

Despite these concerts' success, I thought the audiences we attracted were relatively small and I thought we could do something bigger in future iterations. Eventually, I started to think that we needed to organize a huge concert, unlike any other seen in the Bay Area to that point. I had a Chilean friend who knew the renowned Latino guitarist Carlos Santana, and I told him: "René, is there any possibility that you can help us get in touch with Carlos Santana since you already know him?"

"Sure," he said, "send him some information on the project and I will help you get in touch with him." Back then I was working with the organizing network called New El Salvador Today (NEST), for which I was the special events coordinator. Sure enough, my friend was eventually able to connect me with Santana. When we were finally able to meet in person for the first time, I presented the music icon and his wife a package with information describing the situation in El Salvador, and, especially the circumstances affecting the *campesinos* and their families who lived in areas that were being bombarded by governmental and paramilitary forces. They were very moved. To my great delight, Santana agreed that he would perform at a concert to benefit the children of El Salvador.

Getting Carlos Santana to agree to do a benefit concert for us was exciting; but, in truth, I needed even more than a great artist like Santana to make our large concert concept work: I also needed an experienced producer because it was going to be a huge event. In San Francisco, at that time, "Bill Graham Presents" was the only production company known to mount large concerts like the one we had in mind for Santana to headline. So I went to speak to Bill Graham personally to seek his support. I told him that I wanted his help with the production of the event, and he said, "How many artists do you have?"

"One," I answered.

"One is not enough," he told me. "You need several performers. When you have four or five bands, come and talk to me. I'll help you then."

Through a lot of hard work, we managed to get agreements from a group of seven or eight bands to perform with Santana. Bill Graham honored his commitment and we held the benefit concert on January 20, 1988 at the Henry J. Kaiser Center in Oakland. It was a big gathering, drawing people from throughout the San Francisco Bay Area. I think we had about 20,000 people, and it was a beautiful event. The concert was covered by media throughout Latin America, and my name was mentioned everywhere. It became known in Cuba, Nicaragua and other countries throughout the region. I still have a lot of newspaper clippings documenting the many educational and promotional efforts we supported through the concert, to encourage support for the Salvadoran cause.

After that large success, I continued working with Solidarity. But following the rush and exhilaration of organizing the Santana concert, I experienced some emotional setbacks adjusting to a more normally paced life; and a lot of that had to do with the delayed impacts of all the stress I had put myself through in order to ensure the concert's success. Among the most dramatic manifestations of this, I experienced a severe sciatic nerve flare up and I was bedridden for almost five months. For a time, I literally could not move my legs because of the stress my body had absorbed as a result of my relentless work to organize the Santana benefit. During my healing process, I met many women who worked with Solidarity who treated me with acupuncture. They provided me with a lot of emotional support and medical attention. They helped me to walk again. Largely as a result of their kindness, I am still here.

I recently celebrated my 70th birthday. I remain involved in community work, but now my focus is different because circumstances have changed somewhat and so have I. Much of my focus nowadays is directed to youth education and opportunity. For many years I have worked with the Romero Foundation, named after the late Monsignor Oscar A. Romero, who was assassinated by Salvadoran reactionaries during the height of the violence of the 1980s. We raise funds to support pre-collegiate scholarships for students in various communities throughout El Salvador. Since we began this work, we have been able to assist four high school graduation classes, and some of our students have gone on to graduate from universities. My work now is with the SHARE Foundation, for which I recently traveled to El Salvador to commemorate Monsignor Romero's passing. We took one hundred and fifty delegates. As the years pass and I look ahead to the next stages of my journey, I am increasingly ready to do other types of work.

I will never forget the powerful influences and experiences made possible, however, by my time supporting the struggle for El Salvador's liberty. The transnational organizing work that we supported during this period remains important still today. Organizations like NEST, with which I worked most closely, played essential roles in the service of freedom and democracy in El Salvador. Our efforts in turn were informed by important pre-dating and allied efforts. The Bloque Popular Revolucionario (BPR), for example, was especially well-organized, along with other organizations that informed our work in El Salvador. Sadly, I cannot remember all the organizations that deserve credit. There were so many. At one point in time, I surely could have named these organizations. This is because, for a time, I was in charge of making the banners for all the organizations that we used at our protest marches, both in the United States and in El Salvador. I used a little sewing machine at my home. It is hard to imagine how we found the time and the resources to do all that we did back then. But by virtue of our commitment and what was at stake, we did.

When I first got involved in the work to liberate El Salvador from dictatorship, I participated in endless events; there were a lot of meetings and political activities happening. I would work at a day job in the mornings, to help support my family; and, in the evenings from four to eleven or twelve, I would work on political issues. We would do street organizing and rallies; we would do all sorts of things. So I went through all of that from the beginning until now, where I sit today. Looking back on it all, I feel that I did important and essential work. I feel gratified by the ultimate triumph of our cause.

In the San Francisco Bay Area, and everywhere else that Salvadoran refugees lived, we felt that the war had to come to an end some day. We felt that justice would one day prevail in El Salvador. It did and, gratefully, I was able to bear witness to that historic event because I went to El Salvador to celebrate the peace accords with a Bay Area faction of progressive activists; and we went to Chalatenango. I went with friends from the progressive Farabundo Martí Front for National Liberation (FMLN). We traveled extensively throughout the country during our celebration of the peace accords. I managed to see indicators of all the changes, all the sacrifices, all the work to which I had contributed. And I have continued to remain abreast of the nation's continuing democratic achievements and challenges, because I still travel to El Salvador every year. I go to those places where I contributed so that people could live differently. They now have running water and electricity. They live in a different, improved way in their homes. Of course, not everything is great, but the places that received some of the funds that I helped to raise are markedly better off today because they can at least grow food and pursue other basic things in peace, to survive.

There have been some changes that have taken place for women in El Salvador. They are stronger now, having formed various women's organizations that have allowed them to have a voice and be heard. Their participation is different from many years ago. They have largely left behind the repression under which they lived for years, either at the hands of their father or their husbands. The participation of women in El Salvador is admirable. This is one of the great legacies of my female comrades who lost their lives fighting for a better life for their children. Those children are now different, thanks to the sacrifices of their mothers.

As a Salvadoran woman myself I have experienced the improvements of which I speak here firsthand, even though as an immigrant in California. For a long time, on and off over the years, I have been cleaning the homes of North American people to make a living. That is how I have learned to speak English, but it is also how I have extended the influence and reach of my social justice work, especially in El Salvador. Through my activism, I have successfully encouraged many of my U.S. employers—mostly women themselves—to make generous donations to the various causes I have supported, including most recently the scholarships for students in El Salvador. I am proud of my role as a hardworking woman who has been able to make a difference through dedicated advocacy and organizing.

I am at an age now, however, in which physical labor and non-stop organizing wears me out. That work is not easy. In fact, it is exhausting. Indeed, as a result, after cleaning houses for so many years, I have accumulated many physical injuries. One, related to my shoulder required a major surgery. I was incapacitated for about four to five months. I was concerned because I did not want to feel imprisoned in my house. I like to be active. I had to see what I could do during those months of rehabilitation; I did not just want to sit around the house all day. I did not want to feel useless. These are reflections and sentiments that flow naturally from being a Salvadoran woman and one who has been actively involved for many, many years in the heavy lifting associated with advancing important causes.

When I think about the future of the Salvadoran people, whether in my home town of San Francisco or in El Salvador, I mostly focus on the fact that still today something like two hundred and fifty Salvadorans immigrate to the United States every day. The community over there in the countryside, in the cities, in the neighborhoods remains very impoverished. When traveling in El Salvador, one can see the persistent poverty, the depression due to lack of employment. What has especially created more poverty for Salvadorans is the devaluation of the nation's core currency, the *colón*. There are many organizations that continue to fight for the rights of the poor and that is admirable, that is what we continue to support from here. But, overall, there is relatively little we can hope to change without major economic reforms.

Most Salvadorans who have come to the United States over the past two decades have come because they needed to work in order to support themselves and their families back home. Indeed, in this country, they have found a way both to survive and at the same time to help those they left behind in El Salvador. Many are not politically involved; however, a certain segment of the Salvadoran population here in the United States do not want to lose contact with the political organizations that represented their interests in El Salvador and they do not want to forget why they left their country. At the same time, they want to participate meaningfully, politically and otherwise, in the United States. Unfortunately, a lot of them only have time to work, because there is no other alternative. They have to survive in this country and it is generally not very easy for them to do that; they suffer a lot.

I witness this on a daily basis here in San Francisco, where our predominant Latino population is Central American. Hundreds of immigrants, who not only come from El Salvador but also from other Latin American countries, assemble every day on a street here called César Chávez, beginning at 4 a.m., in hopes that someone—a construction contractor, a homeowner in need of heavy gardening assistance, etc.—will hire them as day laborers. There are times when these immigrants wait there day and night, and yet no one hires them. There is a lot of abuse inherent in making a living that way. Often, contractors will pick them up and have the immigrants work all day long, only to leave them without pay. The immigrants frequently end up working for nothing. And when they try to get their money, they are insulted and threatened that they will be incarcerated, or repatriated by the Border Patrol. This is a very sad situation.

It is generally easier for undocumented women to find employment cleaning houses for $5 or $6 an hour. But, even with that being the case, Central American and other Latin American immigrant families in the United States today are facing increasingly harsh circumstances. There are times when you see them with their children on the streets, sleeping under cardboard boxes. It is a terrible thing to see.

The continuing exodus of Salvadorans I referenced earlier is also occurring because of unfortunate social and political circumstances taking shape in El Salvador today. For example, recent years have seen the development of powerfully organized and highly violent Salvadoran gangs operating both here in the United States and in El Salvador. At times it is hard to know which is worse: the emerging transnational gangs taking hold in the Salvadoran culture or the death squads that wreaked havoc on El Salvador during the 1980s. The rise in gang violence and participation among Salvadoran youth has risen in recent years, in part, because the refugee and immigrant parents of the current generation of Salvadoran teens and young adults were unable to take care of their kids during their formative years. This is because they had to work so feverishly to survive in this country, often working two or three jobs at a time to make ends meet. Because of resulting bad experiences and unhealthy influences here in the United States, these children did not do well in school or the larger society. As their challenges mounted in areas ranging from acculturating to surviving as immigrant youth on the mean streets of big cities like San Francisco and Los Angeles, many became immersed in the gang culture and subsequent Salvadoran community youth have followed in their footsteps.

The Salvadoran gangs that now wreak growing havoc on our community thus started here in the United States and were taken to El Salvador. And now gangs have spread throughout Latin America under the banner of "La Mara Salvatrucha." Salvadorans are now increasingly known across Latin America as a primary importing source of U.S.-style gang violence. It is very painful that Salvadorans are known like that these days because this gang culture is not at all intrinsic to our heritage; rather, it is a manifestation of our dislocation and suffering as a community during the past several decades. Still, our emerging reputation as a violent, criminal people is affecting us a lot.

It would be good to see the governments of this nation and El Salvador do much more to create meaningful alternatives to the proliferation of gangs and related violence where our young people are concerned. I hope that this occurs in the near future because we are losing a whole generation of our youth. If you see the jails in El Salvador, they are full of gang members, of all sorts of young people whose crimes are terrible. There are killers, rapists and abusers of all sorts incarcerated there. It is a vast waste of humanity. But instead of intervening with positive alternatives, the governments both here and in El Salvador merely make matters worse by addressing the problem only with punishment and oppression. They have abdicated the responsibility and opportunity to achieve real change among these youth to private organizations.

Gratefully, there are effective community-based and international organizations that are increasingly playing a role in providing our youth with constructive alternatives to gangs. Organizations like those I have worked with in recent years—the Romero Foundation and the SHARE Foundation, for example—are good cases in point. Of course, there are some young people who do not want help, no matter what you offer them. However, there are many more who do want to overcome their situation and pursue peaceful and successful lives.

One thing that prevents a lot of troubled youth from advancing even when they want to and even when they have sought help is that they often have gang-related tattoos visibly featured on their bodies. This affects them negatively when they apply for employment. A person who is tattooed is never seen positively; rather, they are seen as a gang member and they are easily rejected by possible employers. Here in San Francisco, thankfully, there is an organization called Second Chance and there, they help to remove the tattoos carried by gang members and troubled youth who have experienced difficulties with the law and other institutions. We need to create more programs that help our young to succeed, rather than fall prey to lives of violence and self-destruction. It is essential that we do this if we are to honor all that my generation fought for on behalf of these children during the Salvadoran wars of the 1980s.

When I think ahead to my own future, I tend to agree with my daughter and my granddaughter who often say that in the next ten years or more, I will continue to speak and to sing. I hope I can do both. I really do not see myself sitting in a rocking chair, with a cane. No way, not that for me. I certainly hope that I do not end up like that because I like to travel a lot and when I retire in a couple of years, I would like to travel the world and see other cultures. Although I have traveled quite a lot over the years, I want to travel even more and continue going to El Salvador to see how the projects I helped create are advancing.

Rossana Pérez

My name is Irma Rossana Pérez and I am from San Salvador, El Salvador. My early experiences in life were informed by several events that had a lasting impact on me. The ones that most come to mind occurred when I was about five years old and my family lived in Planes de Renderos. One lasting image that I recall from this time was my family's love of reading and poetry and how we would organize important parts of our lives around literature.

I remember, for example, that I used to love to sit on a rocking chair behind my older sister as she studied. I also recall my father frequently reading to us passages from the writings of Rubén Darío, a Nicaraguan poet. I memorized several of those poems and when I started to go to school, I would recite them. I have very fond and funny memories of this. I was a very short little girl, and my teachers would make me stand on top of a table when I would recite, so that my classmates could see me.

My memories of this time in Planes de Renderos are also informed by a strong sense of nature and space. Planes de Renderos is like a mountain and, at that time, there were not many people living there. It was a child's dream come true to live in such a place, so full of vegetation and vistas of the landscape around San Salvador. I loved to look at plants, to look at the sky, to pass the time dreaming. It was a magical place to grow up.

Another important memory from my childhood occurred when I was about nine years old, in 1969. At that time, the Salvadoran soccer team traveled to compete at a tournament in Honduras. My grandfather loved soccer and so every weekend the only thing that we would listen to on the radio was soccer games. My grandfather was particularly excited about the tournament in Honduras; I believe it was the Central American cup. I remember that, as he listened happily and enthusiastically to one of the games, there was suddenly an announcement about some problems in the stadium, some sort of riot. The conflict escalated and, eventually, it became necessary to call in the military to restore order and escort the teams off the field. The happy and excited atmosphere in our home quickly changed to one of anxiety. As we listened to the broadcast, we could hear people on the radio screaming as the radio broadcaster confirmed that people were being hurt.

Later, on that same day, we heard reports that the Salvadoran military was taking up positions on Honduran lands that they were coming in through Olancho. Olancho is a province in the north of El Salvador by Chalatenango. The reports indicated that the Salvadoran military strongman José Alberto "Chele" Medrano was killing men and brutalizing women along the way. Hearing all that made me scared. It made me feel uncertainty and insecure. I wondered if the Hondurans would retaliate with their military, putting our family at risk. I also intuitively recall feeling a sense of dismay about the instinct in people to address their conflicts through violence.

The conflict between El Salvador and Honduras that began that day came to be known as the One Hundred Hour War. It lasted a couple of days and then it was over. But it really was not over. In some sense, it marked the beginning of even much worse events that would permeate El Salvador for years to come. Chele Medrano would be heavily implicated in this as the recognized founder of rural paramilitary groups that would terrorize the Salvadoran people with the backing of the U.S. CIA and the Salvadoran government throughout the 1970s and 1980s. During my later childhood and early adult years, I and others of my generation watched as the violence grew throughout El Salvador, ultimately escalating into a full blown civil war. Ultimately, like many of my generation, I left El Salvador because of the war. I was twenty-four years old at that time.

The more specific events that led to my leaving the country dated back to the years just following my high school graduation. In 1977, I completed high school. The political situation in El Salvador had become very difficult by that time. There were many protests and strikes being organized, and the ruling government was fighting aggressively to quell labor unions, students and other progressive forces that had organized to challenge its increasingly repressive tactics. *Campesinos* (farmers) were organizing at the national level from the countryside through a group called Unión de Trabajadores del Campo (Union of Countryside worker's, UTC) and other organizations like UTC were also mobilizing in the city as well as in rural areas.

By the early 1980s, in the capital city of San Salvador, professionals, physicians, nurses and other historically non-politicized groups were organizing against the government and in addition lending their moral and financial support to anti-government factions of labor union members and *campesinos*. They were also beginning to demand improvements in their own salary and employment conditions. In response, their employers, conspiring with government interests, would discredit and abuse them. In the most extreme instances, vocal government and business critics would suddenly disappear, or be kidnapped and beaten.

In 1975, there were several brutal massacres committed by paramilitary death squads and military police. The worst of these took place in Cayetana, near Chalatenango. Many people were brutally killed there. As a result of this government-sponsored terror, Salvadorans became increasingly afraid to organize and to participate in resistance efforts for fear that they would be persecuted or assassinated. This was exactly the government's intended consequence of their heavy-handed tactics. All of these things eventually inspired me to become active in the then-emerging resistance movement that mainly involved students and workers groups.

In 1977, after completing high school, I registered at the Universidad Nacional de El Salvador (National University of El Salvador). The following year, I became active with a group of university students called the Asociación de Estudiantes Revolucionarios Universitarios Salvador Allende (Salvador Allende Association of Revolutionary University Students). Salvador Allende had been the popularly elected president of Chile in the early 1970s, before military leaders in that nation, backed by the CIA, assassinated him and took power in a coup that resulted in the assent of General Augusto Pinochet as that nation's military dictator. Our student association sponsored activities with people from the countryside, to support and assist them as best we could in the face of the growing violence that was then becoming prevalent in our nation.

In 1980, partly on account of the progressive opposition activities that were being sponsored by student groups like ours, the Salvadoran military closed the university and took it over. In the process, they brutalized and kidnapped many people. Many others were detained, some of whom we never saw again. The university was not reopened until the early 1990s. During the more than ten years of its closure, the Salvadoran military essentially destroyed the institution. They demolished the library, as well as the most valuable technology and equipment contained in the various departments of study. Many former students and teachers were systematically harassed during this period.

I continued to participate in various popular organizations with friends and colleagues, including my first husband who was very active in the resistance. We felt that we had to do what we could to mitigate the growing repression all around us. But we paid an increasingly high price for our convictions. My husband was disappeared in 1981. Shortly thereafter, I was kidnapped by paramilitary forces and incarcerated in a women's prison, where I was retained until 1983. I was released along with ninety other female detainees as the result of a general amnesty for political prisoners that San Salvador's mayor, Napoleón Duarte negotiated as part of his continuing though sadly unsuccessful campaign to win the presidency.

Upon my release from prison, my parents thought that it would be best if I left the country. They feared that if I remained in El Salvador I would run the risk of being killed. My daughter Sara was two-and-a-half years old at that time. For her benefit, we left the country with my sister. We went to Mexico because the government there had generously granted us a visa. We stayed there with several of my mother's acquaintances for about a month. Frankly, we had no long term plan of any sort when we arrived in Mexico. It was entirely unclear how permanent or fleeting our stay there might be. Our main motivation was to flee from the growing dangers and injustices of life in El Salvador; but what we were running to was entirely unclear to us.

Interestingly, when I arrived in Mexico at the airport there, I ran into an ex-professor, Chino Iván. One of the first questions he asked me was, "Are you staying in Mexico or are you going somewhere else?" I answered him honestly, "The truth is that I don't know if I'm staying here; maybe I'll go on to Los Angeles." I had mentioned Los Angeles almost on a whim. I really did not have any reason to think of California, except that I had heard many Salvadorans were going there. He confirmed this and told me that in Los Angeles some Salvadoran leaders were trying to start an organization for refugees and that it would be good to contact them if I went there.

As it ended up, my sister and I decided to move with my daughter to Los Angeles. This was during the summer of 1983. Ironically, an unanticipated but important factor in our decision was learning through mutual contacts that my late husband's mother had relocated there. I did not really know her, or the rest of his family. But, even if indirectly, we shared an important set of losses and joys—my husband's disappearance and my daughter's birth. Consequently, we made our way to California and located my mother-in-law. She had taken up residence in a downtown neighborhood near the University of Southern California. We lived with her for about a month or two. It was a difficult time for us.

When I would talk to my mother-in-law and ask her if she knew of any Salvadoran refugee organizations, she would strongly discourage me. She would say, "Oh, no, why do you want to get involved with that? Don't you see what happened to you? Why do you want to get involved in more problems?" She did not appreciate how deeply I felt that I needed to find people like me, or how important it was to me and our community to explore possibilities to regain the humanity of our country.

In the end, on my own, I simply started looking for others like me who might be out there somewhere. One day I found myself walking along Pico Boulevard inquiring about where I might locate Salvadoran refugees. Someone I met along the way told me, "Oh, yes, there's a place, a church, called Anglican Lutheran Church on Burlington Avenue." I immediately went to the church in the Pico-Union district of Los Angeles and I was directed to the second floor. There, in a really small room in the back of the building, I met a man named Jaime Flores. When he heard my story, he explained to me that he had been working with a group of other Salvadorans to organize some efforts around community support services and dialogues. He told me,

"Look, we're starting to meet on Saturdays and if you want to come there's a food bank." I said, "Okay, I'll try." In fact, I was very enthusiastic to have found Jaime and potentially others with whom I might find common cause. That is how I started to connect with people from all over Los Angeles who were working in solidarity with Salvadoran refugees and their families back home. This was in August of 1983.

I thought it was important to become active in this work because of my personal experiences and convictions. I had come to this country as a victim of and witness to the atrocities that were being visited on my country's people. I had survived prison, torture and the loss of my husband. I felt strongly that I needed to tell the story of the war. I especially wanted to help U.S. citizens comprehend what was happening in El Salvador and much of Central America, in large part owing to U.S. governmental policy and tacit U.S. approval of official oppression in the region.

My strong impression was that people here in the United States were uninformed about Latin America in general and that they did not thus fully comprehend the connections between the atrocities that were occurring in places like El Salvador and the covert decisions of their own government. As a result, many North Americans incorrectly thought of Salvadorans like me as illegal immigrants merely seeking economic opportunity in this nation. In fact, the Reagan administration's official position not to recognize us as political refugees and effectively encouraged this misinformed view. But I knew that Salvadorans were in fact coming as a consequence of state-sponsored terror that was being supported by the White House. I felt responsible to speak out publicly and to share experiences from that part of my life that gave me insights into an alternative reality.

I felt as if I owed this to the people who had been killed and disappeared in my country. I felt that my story might help to put a human face on the crisis in El Salvador and encourage people to rethink some of their assumptions. I thought that by educating Americans, raising their awareness and encouraging their support to end the war in El Salvador, I could help to end the crisis that had forced so many of my fellow countrymen to flee and come to the United States in the first place.

The timing of my arrival in Los Angeles enabled me to quickly engage with many important and exciting leaders and events. I remember that only a few weeks after arriving in California and connecting with Jaime Flores, I was able to attend the inauguration of Clínica Msr. Oscar A. Romero. Monsignor Romero had been El Salvador's most outspoken critic of government policy and he had gained a huge following among the people most affected by the government-sponsored terror. In 1980 he was brutally assassinated by a death squad, apparently on the orders of Salvadoran paramilitary leader Roberto d'Aubuisson. The Clínica event, to mark the opening of a new community health center for Salvadoran refugees, established an important opportunity for anti-government Salvadorans to honor Monsignor Romero's memory.

At the time of the dedication, I had just moved to a new home with my sister and Sara on Pico Boulevard. I was only beginning to gain my footing in the strange new world of Los Angeles. But the Clínica opening gave me an immediate sense that my decision to come to Los Angeles had been a good one. It was a major gathering of leading Solidarity and Sanctuary Movement leaders and supporters. Many important people attended, including Charlie Clemens, the former U.S. air force pilot who had been leading medical assistance efforts targeted to *campesinos* and other victims of El Salvador's right-wing militia, Don Smith of the Synod of United States and Hawaii Presbiterian Church and Juan Ochoa, who contributed to the early formation of the Comité Santana Chirino Amaya and served as the organization's president. The large turnout and sprit of the occasion was inspiring and somehow reassuring to me. I felt that I was beginning to find a home in Los Angeles.

Juan Ochoa's work with Santana Chirino Amaya was particularly important at the time. Eventually, the organization was renamed the Santana Chirino Amaya Central American Refugee Committee, which in relation with El Rescate was Los Angeles's largest and most important Salvadoran community advocacy organization. The original Comité Santana Chirino Amaya took its name from a Salvadoran man from San Vicente who had been living in Los Angeles. When he was detained by the police and determined to be living here without proper papers, he was turned over to U.S. immigration authorities. They in turn deported him back to El Salvador. Within a month after his repatriation, he disappeared and his tortured body was found a short while later. The committee took his name to lift up a symbolic example of what Salvadorans who were deported by U.S. authorities faced upon their return to El Salvador.

Soon after meeting Juan, I became actively involved in the Comité's work; and in time I assumed a leadership position. A year later, when Juan relocated to Canada, we had elections and I was named president of the committee. I served in that position from 1984 to 1992. When I took over for Juan as the Comité's principal, Juan surprised me by recommending that I use an alias. He told me, "You should choose another name so that you can protect yourself and your family. It will protect you and your family here and your family in El Salvador."

Juan's suggestion to use another name, a pseudonym, seemed strange and unnatural to me at first. But in time, I realized that he was probably right. With the situation intensifying in El Salvador, it entirely made sense to use caution given the increasingly visible leadership I was assuming in the movement. So, I decided to call myself Sara Martínez, and even still today a lot of people know me by that name. I never learned to feel fully comfortable having to hide my true identity in order to do work that could benefit my community; it was like working under cover. Even my daughter, still a little girl then, sensed this was illogical and she would ask me, "Why do they call you Sara if that's not your name?"

Questions like that from my daughter crystallized what a complicated situation we found ourselves in as a community. How do you explain to a ten-year-old that there is a terrible war in your country and that measures like changing your identity are necessary to protect members of your family from being kidnapped and possibly killed? We faced very difficult decisions trying to manage communication with our children about what was really going on and what our role was in it, and so forth. Many of us chose simply not to talk about it with our families. Others of us tried the best we could to explain it all in the most basic possible terms. It was an extremely complicated circumstance for all of us.

In 1992, with the long-awaited conclusion of the peace accords in El Salvador, I sent a long letter to acquaintances and people essentially explaining to friends and colleagues a simple but important fact. "Many of you know me as Sara Martínez," I wrote, "but my real name is Irma Rossana Pérez." I felt it was a declaration that I needed to make to finally cleanse myself of all the worst things I had lived through since becoming embroiled in the war and the resistance movement. To my great surprise, even with the peace treaties being signed and executed, I had continued for some months to live in fear of persecution. So, my public statement to reclaim my true identity was, in a sense, my declaration of freedom. It was my way to regain myself, my authenticity and my integrity in the aftermath of a nightmare in which those things had been at least partially taken from me, or at least seriously threatened.

The opportunity to re-establish my true identity was certainly hard earned. For the many years leading up to that time, I had been involved in nearly non-stop work and sacrifice on behalf of the movement to end the violence and injustice facing average Salvadoran people. I remember so many events that I helped to organize and protest actions that I participated in during these years, whether at MacArthur Park in the heavily Salvadoran Pico-Union district of Los Angeles or at the federal building near UCLA in West Los Angeles.

I remember when six Jesuit priests and their helper and daughter were assassinated in November 16, 1989, we organized a spontaneous vigil at the federal building. We arrived there at sunrise the morning after the tragedy. A large number of people assembled there for a couple of hours. It had been nearly a decade since a similar event occurred in which several American nuns had been raped and assassinated by Salvadoran death squad members, and I was struck by a sense of fatigue among so many of us and our allies in the United States. It seemed sometimes as if the violence would never end and as if there was just very little we could do to stop it.

And, yet, I was impressed and surprised that morning in 1989 at the federal building vigil to see that, although people were tired of the continuing political challenges facing our movement, they came out. Many hundreds of people came to show their humanity and desire for peace; and not only Salvadoran activists, but also thoughtful and committed Anglo Americans who had come to understand and appreciate what we were up against. The federal building vigil for the assassinated Jesuits revealed that a great deal of goodwill had been generated through the years between the community of Salvadorans here and the U.S. community of progressive and religious people that supported us.

We built on that goodwill and regained ourselves to continue in the struggle. For nearly two months, each morning, we returned to the federal building to sing, march and reflect. The people's resilience and commitment really impressed me. Even during the cold mornings we woke up to in November and December of that year, the people came out every day with enthusiasm and grace. It was a beautiful expression of community.

The genesis of this achievement was the Solidarity Movement, which I think was a very strong contributor to the ultimate achievement of peace in El Salvador. This movement built on legitimate respect for the wisdom of American-based Salvadoran refugee leaders. U.S. citizens who participated with us were typically not people who saw us as victims of that armed conflict; instead, they saw us as people who were leading a courageous campaign for peace and dignity. So most of our North American allies came with a special degree of commitment to contribute to our work, rather than a need to control or second-guess it.

The Sanctuary Movement was also an uplifting and essential element of our legacy during these years. Some of the first supporters of the Sanctuary Movement were Gloria Kingsler, Joan de Quatro, Cynthia Anderson and Father Luis Olivares. These leaders had joined the cause by early 1984. Various churches were instrumental in the movement's leadership and success. They put themselves on the line and numerous times even faced off against U.S. federal authorities at the risk of losing their tax exempt status and significant sums in court fines.

Over the years, I presented at hundreds of Sanctuary gatherings at Presbyterian and Methodist churches, as well as Catholic and Unitarian churches, and Jewish synagogues. Valued partners from each of these religious communities, as well as universities, businesses and nonprofit social justice networks helped to advance sanctuary as an essential element of our human rights campaign. After the worst of the civil war was behind us, delegations of these groups mobilized and traveled to El Salvador to provide still-needed economic and medical aid to the people there.

We were blessed to have this quality and depth of North American support for our work. Without it there is little doubt that things would have been even far worse in El Salvador than they got during the war. Those of us from El Salvador who came here as political refugees substantially underestimated how long the conflict would last. We were grossly unprepared for the prospect of a protracted struggle to end the war, which was ultimately what was required. I recall that when I started working in the movement with the refugee committee and then El Rescate and Clínica Romero, the idea among most of the Salvadoran community leadership in southern California was that, at worst, we would be in exile for only a few short years. That was the consensus, that is what we all thought. Of course, the war lasted more than a decade following our arrival to the United States. We could not have sustained our movement over this duration of time without the steadfast commitment of our American allies.

The miscalculation of our likely stay here in America resulted in some awkward adjustments that we all had to face in time. As the years passed, most of us working with Sanctuary and Solidarity started to have children, to plant roots here. By definition, these developments made things more complicated for us; we could no longer just say, "When the war ends, we will leave." The nature and duration of our time here in the United States made it increasingly difficult and undesirable for most of us to return to El Salvador. Even after the war finally ended and many of us quickly seized the opportunity to make plans for a return, when we got back to what had been our country, many of us realized that we had changed. Many of us could no longer seriously entertain going back.

This was an ironic conclusion for many of us to draw, to be sure. During the height of our struggle we fought with all our might over many trips to Washington and Sacramento, to cease U.S. support for the Salvadoran military, to prevent local law enforcement agencies from engaging in refugee-related deportation activities and to gain at least a temporary protection status (TPS) that would enable us to remain and work in the United States until the cessation of the conflict in El Salvador. After years of toil, we prevailed on virtually all of these fronts. And yet, in the end, none of these victories ultimately prepared us for the reality that when the war ended, we would finally decide to permanently remain where we already were.

When TPS was approved in 1990, military aid from the United States to El Salvador was virtually ended. The scale of that support for state-sponsored terror had reached nearly $200 million for military personnel and equipment, and U.S. advisors and trainers. TPS legally enabled qualifying Salvadorans at risk of facing persecution back in El Salvador to benefit from employment and residential rights in the United States for up to eighteen months. The Sanctuary Movement, moreover, succeeded in achieving a number of big city resolutions between 1985 and 1990 that exonerated their local police forces from transferring Salvadoran and other Central American refugees to federal authorities on account of their lack of legal immigration status. In their own right each of these developments constituted a huge victory for our cause. Together, however, they established a simultaneously unlikely and historic set of achievements for our community. Looking back on everything, it is impossible not to feel a certain pride and satisfaction in what we were able to accomplish, given especially the dire circumstances our community faced upon arriving in this country.

My life today involves a very different focus and pace than the days that marked my work at the height of the struggle. I am studying now; I am back in school. I started in 2003. I went back to school because I realized along my way that I wanted to write. I wanted to be able to tell the stories of the many brave men and women that I have encountered in my journey as a social justice advocate over the years. My engagement in community organizing over the past 20 years has made for very arduous and difficult work. It has often meant sacrificing weekends, family time and treasured personal pursuits. Few people who are not involved in this way of living can fully appreciate how difficult it is. And yet, without this sort of sacrifice and without people who are prepared to make such sacrifices it would be impossible to realize social progress and change. It would be impossible to make or change history.

I realized the significance of all this in 2002 when I was organizing domestic employees. I spent a year on street corners, in parks and at bus stops talking to female maids and caretakers, trying to organize them. I saw firsthand the difficulty they have in understanding and wanting to work for their own rights. It is a strange contradiction that very often people who are being exploited and know they are being exploited, nevertheless find themselves unable and unwilling to do anything about it because they feel it is better for them to have something, even if only very little compared to what they deserve, rather than to have nothing.

As an organizer, I learned early on that the organizer's golden rule is that you never do for others what they will not do for themselves. Change can only happen where there exists authentic courage and will to make it happen among those who most need and desire it. My work in organizing over the years thus brought me to a personal epiphany; namely, that I needed to do something different with my life. I realized that I needed to go back to school so that I could gain the skills and the legitimacy to write and organize our history, to tell the stories of the refugees and the workers and the grassroots leaders and the women that I have worked with over the years, who despite their many good works remain voiceless and misunderstood.

I know that many people will merely assert, "Well, if you want to write, go ahead and write." But the truth is that we live in a society where if you do not have the proper credentials, you do not have true access to anything. That is what I discovered when I became involved in 1999, along with Roberto Lovato, Aquiles Magaña, Rodolfo Acuña and Carlos Córdova, in an effort to create the nation's first academic Center for Central American Studies at the California State University at Northridge (CSUN). In working to institutionalize the Center, we all had to contribute to course content and teaching. My course was called "The Changing Role of Central American Women." To my great surprise student interest in the Center's work and courses was astounding from the outset.

We could not anticipate this. Initially, we thought that there were very few Central American students enrolled at CSUN's San Fernando Valley campus; but, early in our first academic year, we realized that in fact there were some 1,300 Central American students at the college. To our great surprise we realized early on as well that many non-Salvadoran people were also interested in our program. Students started to register who were Mexican American, as well as non-Latino students of various backgrounds who were genuinely interested in learning more about the situation in Central America.

The huge demand for the new Center's course offerings found me working as hard as I had in some time. I found that I enjoyed the experience and wanted more of it. But I quickly realized that it was not as simple as that. Wanting more access and opportunity in this exciting new world was not the same as being able to attain it. In the world of the academy what matters most is tenure status. I was employed at the Center only as a lecturer, and a half-time lecturer at that. As a result, I was paid by the hour. In addition, I was not eligible to receive university health benefits and I did not have a right to qualify for tenure or funding to undertake the research I wanted to conduct.

In short, my lack of credentials proved an insurmountable hurdle in relation to fulfilling my passions and dreams. That is why I decided to go back to school and to get my academic papers in order and have access to the opportunities that I consider most important to advance U.S. Salvadoran community research and historical documentation. I consider such work to be vital for the future growth of our community here in the United States; and I also consider it an important mark of my own personal empowerment to successfully pursue my ambitions in this connection, rather than merely accommodating conventional expectations that someone in my position could never really achieve such a goal.

Looking ahead to the future, I think there are many interesting possibilities that await our people, both here in the United States and in El Salvador. Several of our most prominent leaders like Werner Marroquín and Carlos Vaquerano are delegates to the assembly in El Salvador. In Werner's case, he is also a member of the Central American Legislative Parliament. It is very interesting for me to see this sort of dynamic and somewhat unique situation evolving between the Salvadoran leadership in El Salvador and in the United States. We are a very transnational people. We are constantly paying attention to what is taking place over there and how that affects us here, and vice versa. I am optimistic that during the next ten years we will see greater numbers of our people become more politically active, both within our communities here and across international borders extending to El Salvador. We already have seen the election of a Salvadoran mayor in Watsonville, CA named Oscar Ríos and the appointment of former California state senator Liz Figueroa (for many years the nation's highest ranking Salvadoran American elected official), to the California Unemployment Insurance Appeals Board.

I think that we will continue to see significant new Salvadoran American political participation in the years to come, especially among the children of first-generation Salvadoran refugees. Compared to my generation of leaders, these young people will almost certainly be even more active and empowered to participate on school and municipal boards, as well as in key elected and appointed political offices across the state of California. I anticipate that our community will also continue to build our anchor institutions and to develop still additional organizational infrastructure in the years to come.

In addition to organizations like CARECEN, El Rescate and SALEF (the Salvadoran American Leadership and Education Fund), we will evolve other key institutions like the credit bank known as Comunidades Credit Union (Communities). When I was working at El Rescate in 1992, and the peaces treaties were being concluded in El Salvador, we were all running around trying to figure out what it all might mean in terms of the likelihood that many people could soon return to El Salvador. It was not clear what might happen and how the new situation in El Salvador might thus affect the vitality and sustenance of our U.S. communities. We were left sort of frozen, trying to figure out what to do next.

In order to try to clarify the situation, we polled over two hundred community members and we interviewed selected community leaders to see what people thought about returning to El Salvador. A majority of our respondents reported that even despite the peace accords, they had no intention to return to El Salvador. That made us think, if people are not going back, our community needs in this country are likely still to grow. In this thought process, we began to forecast what sorts of critical new services or infrastructure might be appropriate to consider bringing on line to address the now apparent reality that most of our people would remain in Los Angeles.

We immediately thought about creating a credit bank similar to entities we knew about in El Salvador that provided small loans to hardworking entrepreneurs or first-time business owners. So we started to do some research and, by 1994, we presented a charter petition to open a community-based credit corporation. The permit was granted in 1997. So Comunidades was opened and it still exists today after more than fifteen years of successful operation. It lends or services money transactions, targeting students who require tuition assistance, people who want to buy a car and families that regularly wire money home to relatives in El Salvador. In the future, we are likely to see the development of additional financial service offerings through Comunidades, as well as the development of comparable entities.

Where the future is concerned for me personally, I suspect that I will always see myself participating and contributing on the community's behalf in some way. I hope to fulfill my plans to finish school and to write. I would like to teach literature, as well as use my education as a strategic organizing tool for the community. In El Salvador and here, we do not find many Salvadoran women in literature. We need to change that. Also in relation to literature, I would like somehow to play a part in encouraging a more robust transnational exchange in the literature of El Salvador and the United States. I would especially like to encourage in this context comparative analyses of how the armed conflict in El Salvador changed our lives, both there and here.

In the years ahead, I would also like to become more of a role model for younger members of our community who are now emerging and facing important choices about their futures and that of our people. It is important to share with the new generations our experiences and to recount them so as not to forget (or, in some cases, repeat) them.

I hope as well that I can become more involved in efforts to reconstruct El Salvador; I think there is a lot of work still to do there. Those of us here in the United States represent a large and increasingly influential community of Salvadorans. Los Angeles is effectively the second capital of El Salvador. I think we still have to deal with some unresolved issues from our experiences during the 1970s and 1980s. There is still considerable fear that we have yet to bring to the surface and resolve. In this respect, we have lived too long in a culture of silence which must be broken. This happens even within our families. People typically do not speak about the war. They understandably want to forget it. But I think we need to face our unresolved fears before we can move forward in a healthy and sustainable way.

We need to acknowledge and recognize that some families were fundamentally divided by the war in El Salvador. Aside from the effects of the Diaspora that led most of us to Los Angeles, there have been many family ruptures as a result of ideological divides. Looking ahead, we need to realize that it is not about who is on the right or wrong side of history. It is more a matter of understanding the moment in which we live and what each individual can do to help heal the wounds that remain open in our community and in ourselves.

In this connection, thinking about the future, I hope we can focus on the positives. The legacy I think of most, where my own journey is concerned, is that I have three beautiful children and I want them to grow up to be responsible and respectful. I want them to pursue and attain an education so they can gain wisdom and grace in relation to the important realities and history that have shaped our world, sometimes for the worse.

The future that I face, and that we as a people face together, can be a far better one than the reality we encountered in the past, if that is what we commit ourselves to. Our accomplishments as a community that confronted incredible adversity are impressive and uplifting. We have much to build on and to be proud of. Our greatest accomplishments have been the product of our joint efforts with one another and with people of goodwill from other communities with whom we have partnered. Establishing the foundation of our informing community organizations and gains has been a collective effort; it has been the consequence of shared work involving men and women of diverse backgrounds who believed in the possibility of creating a different and better world. We should never lose sight of this.

In closing I would like to recall the names of the many people I met along my journey who inspired me to believe in the best of what people and the world are capable of. By naming them, I acknowledge the hard effort and work that they have offered and continue to offer to the Salvadoran people and to all of humanity: Linda Garret, Salvador López, Juan Ochoa, Oscar Cruz, Salvador Sanabria, Jim Butilier, Michelle Prichard, Roberto Alfaro, Anne Mello, Debbie Benada, Aurora Martínez, Orlando López (also known as Ricardo Cartagena), Yadira Arévalo, Francisco Rivera, Della Baján, Sara Stevens, Matt Wauker, Ricardo García, Javier Huete (also known as Jaime Flores), Guillermo Rodezno (also known as Eduardo González), Alicia Rivera, Bruce Vogman, Cynthia Anderson and Charlie Clemens. I should also recognize the many artists and religious community leaders who helped us in such critical and invaluable ways throughout the heights of our struggle: Richard Gere, Jackson Brown, Bonnie Raitt, Esaí Morales, Robert Foxworth, Fiona Knox, Mary Pimenter, Don Smith and Gloria Kingsler. All of these extraordinary people deserve special gratitude and acknowledgement, because they helped Salvadorans to establish a platform and a dream for a better life in this country.

Carlos Vaquerano

My name is Carlos Antonio Hernández Vaquerano. I come from a large family of eleven children. Among us there were nine boys and two girls altogether, and I was the second to the last of us to be born. I was born in 1960 in a little town called Apastepeque, in the department (state) of San Vicente, El Salvador. My earliest memory is my father's death. I was three when he passed away. As I grew up, I was told that he was an alcoholic and had died from a liver-related illness. I remember the funeral that followed my father's passing. I recall a lot of people standing and talking outside of our house, and suddenly everyone starting to walk together, I believe, to the cemetery. I do not remember my father at all.

My early childhood memories are generally foggy. In fact, thinking back on my life between the ages of four and twelve, I can recall very little. I mainly remember sad things, like the poverty and hunger we faced as a family, especially following my father's death. I had to grow up very quickly as a result of the many related challenges my mother, Leonor, had to confront being a widow and the mother of so many orphaned children. I had to work very early in my life to help our family and I had to confront many social realities that were beyond what small children should have to know about. Given these realities I had to assume adult-like responsibilities from the beginnings of my journey. In spite of this, I also experienced some of the typical things that go with any childhood; I played with wooden toys, like yoyos and tops, as well as marbles, slingshots, bicycles and car tires. I also played soccer, of course.

In my early teenage years I remember government opposition organizations starting to form in the area where we lived. There was El Bloque Popular Revolucionario (the Popular Revolutionary Front, BPR), El Movimiento Estudiantil Revolucionario de Secundaria (the

High School Student Revolutionary Movement, MERS), and Fuerzas Populares de Liberación (the Popular Liberation Force, FPL). These organizations were all related to what ultimately came to be known as El Frente Farabundo Martí para la Liberación Nacional (the Farabundo Martí National Liberation Front, FMLN).

I recall members of the early resistance organizations that predated the FMLN initiating actions and recruiting members in our town beginning in the early 1970s. They used to come and paint the names of their organizations on public walls all around our area, like street graffiti. They also distributed flyers about their organizations. I remember that one of these groups took over the church of our town for several hours one afternoon during this period. The group's leaders put a banner on the top of the church, closed themselves inside and started speaking to the townspeople about the government's abuses, through the church's loudspeakers. All the people who were in the center of town at the time gathered outside of the church to listen. These developments established my earliest awareness of political realities in our country.

Shortly thereafter, in 1972, the presidential elections took place and I remember that election campaign very well. I was twelve years old. My older brother William was already involved with the armed guerrilla resistance by that time, though I was unaware of the depth of his involvement. William was a high school history teacher who belonged to an anti-government teacher's union called La Asociación Nacional de Educadores Salvadoreños 21 de Junio (the National Association of Salvadoran Educators of the 21st of June). This group was emerging then as an early rebel element in the struggle for change in El Salvador, though it had been formed originally as a conventional teachers' union in 1967. As I recall, William oversaw the organization's propaganda efforts. My brothers Marcial, Numan and Osmín were also involved in opposition efforts by this time, though the latter two were younger and just getting started.

Even though our family had never supported El Partido Demócrata Cristiano (the Christian Democratic Party), because it was a moderate-right political party and we were politically progressive, I remember that Marcial carried the party's leader and presidential candidate, Napoleón Duarte, on his shoulders during that 1972 election cycle, at a campaign event near our home. We cheered Duarte on so that he could win because we thought he might be able to affect some social and democratic changes in our country. We were all disheartened when his subsequent apparent victory was annulled by the Salvadoran military.

My older brothers' involvement in the opposition forces that challenged El Salvador's status quo had a significant bearing on my life. Although they never actively tried to involve me in the resistance efforts that were forming at that time—probably out of fear that something bad would happen to me—I found their commitment inspiring. I knew that they were involved in anti-government activities. They would bring friends who were also involved to our house and they would secretly conspire. I never knew the details of their discussions and I was too young to care then anyway, but I did know that what my brothers were involved in was both important and potentially dangerous.

I recall one day shortly after the elections in 1972 when the National Guard came to our town to look for the people who were involved in the celebration of Duarte's victory. Since joining the opposition, my brother William had become a particular target of the police, and so we came to fear that the military would show up at any moment to take him away. Fortunately, William was able to escape without being detected and to find a temporary hiding place in the forest near where we lived.

I remember that incident very clearly because, after that day, William never returned to live with us in our home on a regular basis. Numan soon followed, and then Marcial. Their involvements in the struggle had intensified noticeably during these first few years of the conflict, and they knew that if they continued living at home they would be putting the rest of our lives in immediate danger. Marcial, a university student, had become involved in Los Universitarios Revolucionarios 19 de Julio (the Revolutionary University Students of the 19th of July), a student organization named after a government-sponsored massacre of students and opposition leaders that occurred on that date in 1972.

After my older brothers were forced to leave our home we were able to see them only very rarely. In between their irregular visits we really had no idea where they were. All of this created a situation of uncertainty, fear and tension in our household. We lived in constant fear that one or the other of my older brothers might be apprehended by the military at any time and taken away or killed on account of their involvement in rebel activities.

My brother Numan ultimately became especially active in the armed struggle. He would come home every several months from the guerrilla front, sometimes wet from the winter and fall's evening thunderstorms, and he would not have eaten for days. He was typically famished and exhausted, and would stop by the house just to get something to eat and to rest. I stayed by his side throughout every minute of each visit. He would listen to Radio Habana Cuba on our family's short-wave radio, and I would watch the intensity of his reactions to the news reported there. Though he rarely spoke during these broadcasts, his body language suggested that they made him think very profound thoughts. When the broadcasts ended, I would ask him naïve and confused questions because I did not understand what was going on. He would explain it all to me. These exchanges had a large influence on me. Numan was very intelligent.

I graduated from high school in 1979, and I recall that in the period just before I graduated I too became involved in several progressive and anti-government organizations such as neighborhood committees, student organizing efforts, BPR and MERS. I thus began associating with rebel sympathizers and getting acquainted with and passing out opposition informational materials around this time. I was not alone. Many other young people were getting involved during this period, some clandestinely, others much more openly. One of my great motivations to become actively involved in the resistance effort, aside from my older brothers' example, had to do with me personally experiencing social injustice through government policies that discriminated against the poor.

An example of the government's inequitable policies was a legal requirement to pay for and pass an entrance exam in order to be admitted to public high school in our country. The exams were very expensive for poor and low-income families like mine. In addition, they were written at a level that ensured most poor students who had attended public elementary schools would not have the necessary skills to pass. Recognizing this, many poor young people in El Salvador began to organize around this time to end the established system of high school entrance exam requirements. MERS was formed at this time to challenge the national exam system's inequitable impacts on poor students and their families.

One of MERS' strategies was to organize student protests and walkouts, thus involving affected students themselves. In one of the organization's early efforts to challenge the system, however, its principal participants were brutally repressed with state-sponsored violence. Many of the youth were killed. As resistance efforts emerged in response, more state violence followed. The military would frequently come in with tanks and take over schools. Shortly before my high school graduation, the military exercised such a takeover at the Instituto Nacional Salbelio Navarette de San Vicente, where I studied. One Monday morning when my friends and I went to class, we found blood everywhere. It was a horrible sight. It turned out that the army had come over that prior weekend and taken over the school, killing several pro-MERS students they had kidnapped along the way, including some of my classmates. To protest the massacre of our friends, many of the surviving students, including me, walked out of our graduation ceremony.

This was a period of deep difficulty and uncertainty for the young people of my town. Apastepeque had come to be informally known as "Cuba." Government officials and their military cronies had started to label our village that way because our population was largely supporting the growing national liberation movement that included peasants, teachers, students and even some members of the middle class. In fact, our community housed many revolutionaries. We associated with the characterization of our town as a politically progressive place and, in time, we proudly adopted the name "Cuba" for ourselves.

By 1980, organized para-military death squads (Escuadrones de la Muerte), supported tacitly by the national government and trained by U.S. military advisors, had already killed many of my friends who were active in the resistance. They would come to our neighborhood one or two times a week in the middle of the night and select a random group of people, most of them very young, to interrogate. These young people would be kidnapped out of their homes and, in most cases, they would show up dead a few days later, their bodies thrown openly onto the streets.

The death squads' psychological warfare tactics were intense. "Orejas," or government informants would circulate rumors that the army was coming on a given evening, and we would all leave our homes to sleep in the forest so that we would not be kidnapped and killed. In the morning, when we returned home, we would find out that the army had not come after all. The informants spread these rumors night after night to ensure that our local townspeople were living in a state of constant fear, confusion and ultimately exhaustion. Finally, on nights when the army was not supposed to be coming and we would all be comfortably sleeping at our homes, the death squads would instigate surprise raids, taking people away seemingly at random to torture and kill them. Their dead bodies would later be left in the streets.

Most people involved in any way with the anti-government opposition stopped sleeping at home altogether during this time in order to avoid the death squads, and many, like my older brothers, simply moved away or went underground to protect themselves. My youngest brother Osmín and I still lived at home during this period; but all of my other siblings had already moved out and only my mother and grandmother, a couple of my brothers—Fredy, Ricardo and César—and my sisters remained inactive in anti-government efforts. Even Osmín was becoming more and more involved in the struggle, and the recent death squad killings all around us had also begun to push me towards a more active participation in the resistance.

Knowing this, my mother became especially concerned for all of our safety during this period. I remember that she would sometimes tell me, "Son, go sleep in the forest. Don't stay here because if they find me here, they won't do anything, but if they find you they will kill us all." For months and then years following my mother's admonitions about sleeping in our home, Osmín and I mainly slept in other friends' houses or in the nearby forest so that we could protect our more vulnerable family members from the violence and the madness that was overtaking our country. Unfortunately, our precautions did not help to spare my mother and our family from tragedy.

On July 12, 1980, a death squad mission found its way to Apastepeque. My brother Marcial, a university student and an active member of the anti-government rebel group Fuerzas Populares de Liberación, or FPL, had unexpectedly come home from San Salvador for the weekend. On the afternoon of the 12th, Marcial and I talked about the struggle and the situation that our country was facing. I wanted to learn from him what was happening and to offer my support and admiration of his courage. Marcial and I used to fight with each other over little things, just like any other brothers; our relationship was uneasy during those days. But that afternoon, we had the best—and last—time of our lives together. I actually did not know the level of his involvement until that afternoon when I saw that he had a gun. In those days, when the armed resistance was just beginning to form, to have a weapon meant that you were deeply involved.

Our town's annual Saint's Day celebration had begun, and there were many people and activities being assembled at our local park. So, after spending several hours at home, Marcial and I decided to take a break and walk to the park to hang out with our friends. On the way, we talked about our cousin Luis who was also involved in the rebel FPL. After spending a few minutes at the park, I decided to leave Marcial there with some acquaintances in order to visit our other brother, Fredy, at his home. I used to visit Fredy every evening to listen to music. I have always liked music. At Fredy's home I settled in as usual, listening to various recordings, and talking to him and my sister-in-law. About a half hour following my arrival at Fredy's place, however, a group of masked men dressed in paramilitary gear passed in front of the house. It was certainly a death squad. Its members were all heavily armed.

Our mood shifted quickly from lightness to grave concern. People around the neighborhood started to close their doors and windows. The collective fear that followed the death squad's footsteps was evident. The armed death squad members assembled around our town's two sole entrances in order to prevent anyone from leaving. Within several minutes, some surrounding neighbors and townspeople began screaming. The first thing I thought about was Marcial. I realized that Marcial was extremely vulnerable. In the first place, I knew that he was unarmed. I also knew that with the festivities occurring at the local park his guard was down. Finally, I knew that Marcial was not accompanied at the time by anyone who might be able to protect him should he be apprehended by the approaching death squad.

The whole situation was unsettling. Before we left my mother's home earlier that afternoon, Marcial had asked me to hide his pistol under our grandmother's bed pillow. I had done that. Consequently, under the circumstances, if our house was later searched and that weapon revealed, it could very well result in our entire family's murder. At the time, a death squad finding a hidden gun like that in a private home usually resulted in a slaughter of the entire family. Thinking over all of these things made me feel very distressed.

About an hour later, my aunt Carmela came to tell us that the death squad had kidnapped Marcial and seven other men, including my cousin Luis. I asked her if the death squad had been to our house. She did not know, but she urged me to spend the night elsewhere, where I could better ensure my safety under the circumstances. I begrudgingly followed her advice and spent the entire night at Fredy's home wondering what had happened to Marcial and the others. I did not sleep at all that evening. I was sick and terribly sad. So was Fredy. We nervously pondered what might happen next. Was the death squad going to come for us, too? Were they going to go to our family home and find Marcial's gun there? Were all of us soon to be killed?

At five o'clock in the morning I got out of bed and went straight to my mother's home. It was crowded with neighbors. Everyone who lived on our street was at our house. Following my arrival, my mother and grandmother confirmed that the death squad had kidnapped eight young men. Among those apprehended were Marcial, our cousin Luis, and Marcial's brother-in-law, Meme. It was a very frightening and emotional moment for my mother. Several neighbors and friends tried to console her, but she was overcome with grief.

After a few minutes, making sure I was alone and not followed, I walked into my grandmother's bedroom and I went directly to her bed and looked under her pillow. Marcial's pistol was still there. I thanked God. Later on, I found out that after the death squad kidnapped my brother, they had also passed by my mother's home to look for me and my brother Osmín; but we were able to avoid the worst by not being there at the time. Much to my dismay, I also learned that my mother and my grandmother had been forced to face the death squad and their brutal interrogation and intimidation tactics that afternoon. When the death squad came to the house, they promptly threw the women to the ground. They ransacked the house, taking out all my mother's and grandmother's clothes from their closets and dressers. They were clearly looking for guns. It was a miracle that they did not have the instinct to check under the pillow in my grandmother's bedroom. As a result of this stroke of good fortune, the intruders did not find anything incriminating.

When I recovered Marcial's gun from my grandmother's bedroom, I hid it in my clothes. My brother Osmín came to me and asked, "You know where the gun is?" Osmín was short-tempered and did not think things through sometimes. I showed him the gun. "Here it is," I said.

Osmín then took the gun from me and said something I will never forget: "With this gun, I will avenge my brother."

While we still could not be sure, we were fairly certain that the death squad was going to kill Marcial that evening, if they had not already done so. When I returned to resume conversation with our assembled family members and friends, my mother begged me, "Son, you have to leave." I agreed with her. It was clear that if I did not leave immediately, I would be running a very dangerous and unnecessary risk. I would also be further threatening my mother and my grandmother's safety. That is why that very day, on July 13, 1980, I left Apastepeque for San Salvador, where I stayed for a time with relatives of Marcial's girlfriend who were then living in the capital. I was accompanied by Meme's cousin, Mario.

In San Salvador, the same afternoon that we arrived, our neighbor Maura came to visit us from Apastepeque to tell us that Marcial's body had been found with six others. They had been massacred, assassinated. My cousin Luis was found a week later, brutally killed, his dead body hanging from a bridge. All of the deceased young men had been treated harshly indeed on their way to being killed. The death squad had pulled off their victim's fingernails and severely beaten them in each case, leaving them barely recognizable. They had been burned with acid, moreover, and shot in the head. Our neighbor Maura further informed us that my brother had been taken to El Playón, the place where death squad members dumped the cadavers of the people they killed. Marcial and the others had been laid out in a row, one by one, for broad public display.

The impact of this horrible news on our family was devastating. Aside from feeling a massive loss with the confirmation of Marcial's killing, it was very frustrating not being able to be with my family at such a time, owing to the danger still all around us. My mother, mindful of these realities, asked me to not visit; she did not want me to meet the same end that Marcial had. It was a very difficult situation. I learned that Marcial and the others who had been killed along with him were buried together; thousands of people attended the funeral.

My brother Osmín was hanging around the area, but he could not attend Marcial's burial because the military were now also looking for him. Our brothers Fredy, Ricardo and César were sufficiently free of risk at that time to attend the burial. One of my sisters, who was living in San Salvador, also attended; we still expected the death squads to respect women at that time. The rest of us, however, were unable to attend Marcial's last rites of passage due to security considerations.

The entire situation was terrible for our family and loved ones. It also remained very dangerous for us in the days and months that followed Marcial's killing and burial. We knew that it might not be a good idea to resume our lives in the area. Shortly after Marcial's very public burial, therefore, my mother and my grandmother decided to leave our home for Chalatenango where one of my sisters had a home. I accompanied them. Later we all moved into my brother César's home in Ilobasco. After that, we came back to San Salvador. Altogether, we spent about two-and-a-half months fleeing.

During this time I was faced with a fundamental dilemma: should I stay and continue living in a country steeped in the kinds of risks that had resulted in the murder of my brothers and so many others, or should I continue with my studies in some other country where I could be much safer? My goal then was to study medicine, and, with that in mind, I had graduated high school with a focus on science. This was 1980, however; and that was ironically the year when the Universidad Nacional was taken over and then closed by the Salvadoran army. The university shut-down was part of a military campaign of the government to intimidate students and others aligned with the guerrilla forces or the FMLN.

These developments helped to seal my fate. I would have to leave El Salvador. In the circumstances of the time, I really had no other option. I could not go to the university, which had been indefinitely shut down. I could not go back to my mother's home without the risk of being tracked down there by the authorities for retaliation. My brother's murder, the other senseless killings that were taking place all across El Salvador, the assassination of the head of the Catholic Church, Monsignor Oscar A. Romero on March 24—all of these things made clear to me that my country was in a dangerous cycle of violence and despair. I had to get out.

Fortuitously, one of my sisters, Lupita, had found her way to the United States in recent years and she offered to help me to come live with her there for a time in Los Angeles. Making this happen would require a good deal of creativity and ingenuity, because I had no papers to gain a legal right of passage to the United States, and also because I had little money to finance my way to Los Angeles. These were somewhat steep obstacles, especially for an individual and family with such relatively limited means; but, with the help of family and friends, we took care of everything right away.

We found a way to get the money and the contacts to help me cross the U.S. border. I was able to fly from San Salvador to Mexico City, where my brother-in-law's relatives offered me assistance. The hardest thing was to leave my family in El Salvador. My biggest concern was my mother; I have always been very close to her. I knew she was in a very difficult situation with virtually all of her sons now facing the possibility of death at any time. With my brother Marcial's murder, most of my brothers stepped up their engagement in armed opposition activities. I thought my leaving the country increased the possibility of sparing my mother another heart break. I also thought my decision to go to the United States would ultimately help my mother and family by enabling me to earn money that I could send back home from time to time. This all turned out to be true in my case. Sadly, things did not turn out so well for my other brothers who remained in El Salvador.

Before I left to make my way to Los Angeles, my brother Numan, who was now very involved in the FMLN, came to visit me in San Salvador. We saw each other only briefly because he was traveling and working in a clandestine manner. I will never forget that day. He said, "I know that you're leaving, and that's good; we have no other alternative. But, don't forget that you have to come back to your country. Never forget that you have to fight so that justice prevails in our country." He told me that there was a growing movement of people in the United States trying to do something against the war. He encouraged me to get involved. And that is how he said goodbye to me. We hugged and cried for a while; and he left. I never saw Numan again.

I left El Salvador on October 12, 1980, on my twentieth birthday. Several close family members and friends took me to the airport, including my mother and some of my nieces. I clearly remember all of us crying when the moment came for me to board my flight. This made leaving an especially sad occasion for me. It was also a frightening moment. Once I boarded my plane, I was entirely alone. I had never felt that way before in my entire life. I arrived in Mexico and stayed there with my brother-in-law's relatives for about three weeks.

I learned how to be comfortable enough in Mexico City, but my goal was to leave as soon as possible and make my way to Los Angeles. In order to make the journey north, however, I would have to perfect an illegal passage, like so many Mexican immigrants to the United States. People I met in Mexico City taught me how I could make it across Mexico and arrive safely at the U.S.-Mexico border in Tijuana. They taught me new words and phrases to help me present myself as a Mexican and negotiate my way through the system. They also helped me to secure a bus ticket to Tijuana, a falsified Mexican birth certificate and provisions to sustain myself on the long journey north.

When I left Mexico City, I had an uneventful but, nevertheless, anxious ride to Tijuana. My brother-in law's brother who was a driver for an inter-state bus company offered to take me from Mexico City to Tijuana as his assistant. That was a façade; I just had to pretend to be the "assistant." We drove several days, passing through Guadalajara and finally through the city of Tuxpan, in the state of Nayarit. I stayed there for approximately five days to rest and then departed to Tijuana. As we approached the U.S.-Mexico border, we came to a Mexican immigration checkpoint. I was asked to get off the bus and to see an immigration agent. I acted confident, but I was actually quite nervous making my way over to the Mexican immigration agent's desk. After a brief exchange of greetings and introductions, the agent started to interrogate me. He wanted to know where I was from and where I was going. I told him that I was from southern Mexico, where the regional accents are similar to the Salvadoran accent.

Everything seemed to go well enough after that. The agent and I talked easily for several minutes. But something must have raised his suspicions. At the close of the interrogation, the agent asked an attending police officer to search me. To my surprise, he looked at the brand of my shirt and found a tag that read: "Made in El Salvador." They asked me if I was from El Salvador. Without thinking, I said, "Yes, I'm from El Salvador." Realizing my mistake I quickly started to explain what I had been through. I told the agent and the police officer that I was fleeing El Salvador as a political refugee and I asked them to help me, to let me through so I could make my way to Los Angeles to find my sister there.

The Mexican officials expressed little sympathy. Their response suggested they could care less about my predicament. They started to confer, I suspected about ways to deport me back to El Salvador. At that point, I took out a $100 American bill and gave it to them as a payment to let me pass. The money had been provided to me in El Salvador by my family. In those days, one hundred U.S. dollars in Mexico was like a thousand dollars nowadays; it was a large sum. I gambled on the hope that the Mexican officials would let me through in exchange for the opportunity for each to walk away with fifty bucks. I figured anyone in their position would have let me through for that kind of money. Thankfully, I was right. They pocketed the $100 and waved me on.

Following my brush with repatriation by the Mexican immigration agents, I made my way to Tijuana. There, I met another group of people who had arrived from El Salvador and other places. I had been told to look for this group so that I could coordinate my border crossing with them and increase my prospects for a successful passage. I did everything the *coyotes* (smugglers) responsible for our illegal entry in the United States told me to do. They assembled us in teams. In my group, there were two *coyotes*, myself and another Salvadoran young man. The four of us crossed the border in a GMC pick up truck at around midnight.

The journey had taken a toll on me. I was exhausted by the time we embarked on the crossing to the States. I was quite short and skinny back then. I weighed only about 100 pounds. As a matter of fact, I remember that when I was little, my friends used to call me "pin," because I was so thin. As we headed towards the U.S. border, I wondered if I was going to make it. I wondered if I would be able to hold up. The conditions of the passage were harsh. The other Salvadoran migrant and I were both placed under the truck's hood in order to camouflage our presence. I was positioned face down over the engine on a towel the *coyotes* had laid there so that I would not burn; nevertheless, it was an extremely hot, uncomfortable and dangerous placement. The other person who accompanied me was made to half-sit in the area around where the truck's battery was located.

Under the circumstances, my slight build turned out to be a great advantage. Had I been a larger man, I am not sure that I could have withstood the time spent in such an uncomfortable and precarious position. Altogether, we were forced to remain in the engine cabin of that truck for nearly half an hour until we made it to the immigration post. That half hour was endless because the truck engine was running the entire time as we made our way through the long line to cross the border. It became unbelievably hot under the truck's hood with each passing minute, and we were getting desperate. It was dark, we did not know what was going to happen, and we had no way of being able to communicate with one another or our clandestine drivers.

At one point in the passage, the truck just sat idle in the staggering heat for maybe eight or ten minutes. I remember telling myself, "If this car does not move in the next few seconds, I'm going to scream!" I did not think I could handle it anymore. Thank God, we finally made it through. I heard the signal. Prior to making our way to the border crossing the *coyotes* told us that they would tap the dashboard when we had successfully crossed the border. And that is what they did a few short minutes after the U.S. border patrol agent gave our pick up the go-ahead to proceed north. Once safely across the border checkpoint, we felt the truck come to a stop. One of the *coyotes* got out of the truck and hastily opened the GMC pick up's hood. We got ourselves out of the engine cabin and jumped into the back of the vehicle. The *coyotes* then took us to a safe house in Chula Vista where one of their families lived. We spent the night there. It was November 4, 1980—nearly a month since I had left El Salvador.

Getting to the other side of the border and out of that engine cabin was like getting a new lease on life. I treasured every breath of fresh air my lungs could take in. I relished simple things in ways I never had before, like my first cup of coffee after the long journey and the refreshing shower I took at our host's home on the evening prior to heading out for Los Angeles the following day. Little did I know that my sacrifices were still not entirely behind me.

On the way to Los Angeles, we had to cross another immigration checkpoint at San Clemente. This time, the *coyotes* put me and the other Salvadoran refugee traveling with us in a small car, one of those in which the back seats fold down. We both crouched down in the back of the vehicle and quietly hoped for our continuing safe passage to Los Angeles. Fortunately, we made our way through the border checkpoint with no incidents. To celebrate our success, we decided to share a long lunch. Ironically, the *coyotes* in charge of our journey took us to a McDonald's. It was a dubious dining decision from my standpoint.

I had only begrudgingly come to the United States to spare my mother and my family more pain and hardship; and I had come with a decidedly anti-American mentality. McDonald's, a symbol of U.S. cultural and economic domination, clearly would not have been my chosen dining establishment for the meal. At first, I stood on principle; I did not want to eat at McDonald's because in my mind it represented the U.S. government that had been supporting the people who had killed my brother and other innocent people in El Salvador. Given my perspective and anti-American thinking then, I was very angry at this country. I was angry at everything and deeply frustrated. At the same time, I was hungry and I had almost no money left to be picky about where to get my next meal. So, I ate the food at McDonald's. I had no other choice.

The day of my arrival in southern California, I went immediately to my sister's home in Van Nuys, in the San Fernando Valley. It was wonderful to reconnect with my sister Lupita and to have a safe and friendly place to land after such a tumultuous journey. I quickly began to look for work, both to survive and because I had to send money back home to my mother and family members in El Salvador. My sister helped me a lot. She provided both emotional support and helpful assistance to get me started in this country. Like many undocumented Latino immigrants, the first jobs that I took were quite menial. I found employment as a day laborer cutting lawns and trees, laying roofs and doing basic construction for nearly a month, perhaps more. Then, my brother-in-law Manuel helped me to get a job at an airplane manufacturing plant.

During this time, I took English classes because my goal was to continue studying. But out of a continuing concern for what was happening in my country, I also began to get involved in Salvadoran community work shortly after arriving in Los Angeles. This made pursuing and completing the studies I had planned very difficult. I made a practice of searching for people who were involved in the Salvadoran community. I would come to downtown Los Angeles, to Broadway, specifically to seek people out. I would take the bus all the way from Van Nuys to downtown Los Angeles—usually more than a two-hour ride.

In early January 1981, after I had been in Los Angeles a couple of months, the first major offensive of the FMLN was reported widely in the local and national press. I came downtown because there were reports that pro-FMLN refugees were gathering to celebrate the attacks. Someone told me about MacArthur Park. They told me that Salvadorans often congregated there and that I should go there to see what might be happening. So, I found my way to MacArthur Park and was elated to find a large march in progress with people waving flags from El Salvador and the FMLN. I ran into my cousin Tano there. That was my first major connection with the U.S.-based Salvadoran political community. I became involved right then and there in helping to advance the community's development and political identity in this country. I have not stopped being involved in this work since.

I became actively involved in social justice work mainly because I had witnessed firsthand the many injustices that the majority of people in my country were being subjected to, such as cruel poverty and repression. We were poor ourselves. I had lived in the shadow of such injustices and experienced personally its worst aspects: the assassinations of my brother Marcial, of my friends, of school classmates, of social heroes like Monsignor Romero. All of that moved me; and, as a result, I think I came to the United States with a clearly defined commitment to become involved in social justice work. That is what drove me to become so heavily involved in the anti-war movement very soon after my arrival in Los Angeles.

When I arrived in the United States, my first priority was to get involved in anything that had to do with the peace movement. I wanted to help in any way possible to defeat the military dictatorship in El Salvador. That was the minimum that I could do to make a difference, and to pay tribute to my brother Marcial, my friends and the thousands others who had been killed by then. My first major engagement involved helping to organize a local chapter of El Comité Salvador Farabundo Martí. I ended up in charge of organizing all of the committee's work in the San Fernando Valley. I got more and more involved with each passing day. I was young and an idealist back then; we all were. More than anything we were driven by the reality that people, many of whom we knew, were dying in the war back home. This had an incredibly galvanizing affect on our work.

We started organizing events to raise funds for the resistance movement, such as rallies, cultural gatherings and informative meetings every Sunday morning called Plenarias. In addition, every week, we would all make tamales to raise money to send back to our country. I remember folding hundreds of tamales while we were sharing sad stories or jokes, and listening to revolutionary music. Once our tamales were made, we would go to local parks, apartment buildings and soccer games to sell them for 50 cents or $1.00. In one hand we had the tamales and in the other we had informational materials to educate people about the war. In time, those *tamaleadas* became a very effective organizing vehicle for us.

My commitment to this work was complete and it only increased as the conflict in El Salvador advanced. I felt very compelled to continue with the work, and my intent was to return to my country and even to sacrifice my life, if necessary, as part of the armed struggle, in order to contribute to the cause. But circumstances ultimately stopped that from happening. An especially important factor that prevented my return to El Salvador was my family. They would tell me, "It's better if you stay over there; you are safe there. If you come back, you can get killed."

But another part of the equation where my family was concerned was the reality that I was the second youngest son in a family that was beginning to lose members to the conflict. By 1981 we had lost my brother Marcial and my brother Numan, who died in combat and whose body was never found. Still later in 1987 my youngest brother Osmín was assassinated while walking on the streets of San Salvador.

My mother was devastated with all that was happening. I don't know how she handled all the pain that she had to endure during those years or where she found the strength to go on. But I believe that in my case, ironically, being removed from the conflict was an important gift to my mother, as well as my other relatives in El Salvador. My being in Los Angeles, it turned out, was comforting to them because, as long as I was in California, they knew that I could be both very active in the peace movement and yet reasonably spared from the worst of the violence that was rocking El Salvador.

For me, the arrangement was frustrating. Being in the United States effectively meant that I could not go back to El Salvador. My response to the killing of my brothers was to get more deeply involved and committed to the cause. Staying involved in the struggle for social justice and peace made me feel closer to home and to my family. Between 1984 and 1991, I was one hundred percent engaged in antiwar activities, working largely without pay. At that time, my colleagues with the El Comité Salvador Farabundo Martí asked me to move to San Diego to help lead our emerging organizing and Sanctuary Movement work there. This forced me to learn English because I had to live with an Anglo family, and also because I had to take on greater public responsibilities given my new assignment.

My role in San Diego was to go to churches, schools and universities where I would speak to student and religious groups. I would share with them my personal testimony, and explain to them how much the people in El Salvador were suffering. We had to create awareness of the U.S. government-sponsored atrocities that were being perpetrated in El Salvador. And that is what many people like me did. I lived in San Diego doing this work for two years and I spoke to thousands of people. It was a very painful experience for me, since I had to speak about the killing of my brothers and friends. I cried countless times before small and large audiences. I just could not stop. Thank God people were very supportive and understanding. Up to this day I still have to deal with war trauma, to the point that when I talk about my brothers I break up crying.

As my journey continued, I started to become more active with the Sanctuary Movement. I remember that around that time I went to a convention in Phoenix, Arizona. It motivated me to become more engaged on the U.S. side of the equation, to help Salvadorans who had come to the United States to seek relief from the violence and persecution in El Salvador by providing them with safe haven and protection from repatriation. With a North American friend named Donald, I helped to start the Centro de Información Centroamericana (Central American Information Center). Basically, we informed people of what was happening in El Salvador and surrounding nations, and we raised funds for direct assistance to Central American refugees here in the United States, as well as key organizations in El Salvador that were trying to help advance justice from that end.

While living and working in San Diego, I had a very scary incident. In late 1984, after the U.S. military experienced a serious terrorist attack in Lebanon that killed or injured hundreds of troops, there was a lot of animosity directed toward people from the Middle East all across the nation. Some of the worst of this anti-Middle East sentiment could be found in Southern California, which remains even today a largely conservative region. During this period, I was flying back to San Diego from a meeting in Los Angeles and I was stopped by three undercover LAPD officers at Los Angeles International Airport. Based on my physical appearance—my dark skin and hair, etc.—they presumed that I was Middle Eastern. I overheard one of the detaining officers surmise that I was probably from Libya. The officers started to interrogate me, searching my briefcase and asking senseless questions. They were unnecessarily rough and intimidating. It was a humiliating and disturbing experience for me, one that for me was more reminiscent of what I had known in El Salvador than what I had ever expected to find in this country.

After several hours of interrogation and intimidation, the police officers naturally learned that I was from El Salvador. Extending their psychological abuse, they threatened to deport me on the spot. They said, "You know what's going to happen if we send you back, don't you?" I kept silent the whole time and that infuriated them. Finally, after finding no evidence of wrongdoing, they let me go. Immediately after my release I got so nervous that my entire body began to shake uncontrollably. I couldn't stop shaking until after my friends had picked me up at the airport and taken me home.

In 1986, I came back to Los Angeles to work with a group called El Comité de Refugiados Centroamericanos (the Central American Refugee Committee), or CRECEN. The organization was established, on the one hand, to assist and organize the Salvadoran refugee community to advocate for political asylum rights in the United States and, on the other hand, to support those who had been displaced within and around El Salvador owing to the war. The organization was born of some of the earliest collaborations on the issues involving leaders from religious organizations, unions and other progressive groups.

Even as the conflict in El Salvador waned toward the end of the 1980s, those of us involved in the anti-war movement here in the United States faced sustained and even increasing threats from home for the peace and justice work we were advancing here. Just before six Catholic Jesuit priests were viciously murdered in El Salvador by death squad vigilantes in November 1989, for example, I remember that many U.S. Salvadoran community leaders, including me, started to receive death threats. Soon thereafter, several of us began to experience real violations of our physical well being. This presented a new dimension and challenge to our struggle. Some leaders' cars were vandalized. One female activist was brutally raped by men who presented themselves as pro-Salvadoran government operatives. So this became an especially dangerous and scary time for all of us.

In response to the rise in threats that I and others began to receive around this time, I decided to start using Vaquerano more often, my maternal last name, as my formal family name here in the United

States. Prior to this I had always used Hernández, because one is generally known in El Salvador by their first last name, the lineal reference to one's paternity. I felt I could mitigate my vulnerability to retaliation and targeting this way. So that is how I came to be known as Vaquerano. Still today, most people only know me as Carlos Vaquerano.

In 1989, the war was beginning to show signs of an impending resolution, but there was still much to be done in the work that I was involved in. After several years of waiting, I was granted permanent residency status through the 1986 Immigration Reform and Control Act, which enabled me to legally remain and work in the United States. With my residency status favorably resolved I was thus able to safely travel outside of the United States without losing my legal standing to return and continue where I had left off. Almost immediately thereafter I traveled to El Salvador. I had been living in exile for nine years by that time. I stayed with my family in El Salvador for almost two months. It was especially gratifying to be able to spend time there with my mother and siblings after such a long absence. During my visit, I also laid the foundation to expand my political organizing activities focused on human rights. Based on this work, I later started to take delegations of religious people and peace activists to El Salvador to investigate the human rights violations committed by the Salvadoran government and military.

Shortly after returning to the United States, I was temporarily redeployed to Washington, DC to help advance concern for El Salvador and related refugee community issues in the national policy arena. For over a year I worked to promote our anti-war and peace agenda in consultation with members of the U.S. Congress. Through our lobbying efforts, we put a lot of pressure on congressmembers to stop supplying military aid to El Salvador's recalcitrant government. This experience helped us learn how to work effectively with Congress to achieve our goals.

In time, as the worst of the war in El Salvador began to come to an end, and it became clear that many Salvadorans in Los Angeles intended nevertheless to remain in the United States, we changed the name of our organization from the Central American Refugee Committee to the Central American Resource Center (CARECEN). The name change reflected the reality that our status in this nation had begun to change. No longer were we merely short-term, asylum-seeking transients in U.S. culture, but rather a growing new permanent community in this country.

After seven years of doing full-time voluntary work for the peace movement, I returned to Los Angeles at the end of 1990, and I started working with CARECEN as a paid employee. This was an interesting development. CARECEN, and its predating sister organization CRECEN, with which I had spent many years as an activist in Los Angeles and Washington, had emerged in recent years to become one of the nation's most active and successful Central American community organizations.

My connections with the organization ran very deep. For several years beginning in 1986, while working as a volunteer for CRECEN overseeing its work in Los Angeles, I had served on the organization's board of directors. Coming back to the organization in a paid staff position and in its then-new incarnation as CARECEN was an important new experience for me. During this period, I served as their Director of Community and Public Relations. In this role, I was able to participate still further in shaping critically important policy developments occurring both in El Salvador and also, increasingly, in Los Angeles.

The year 1992 was an especially important transition for the Salvadoran community in both contexts. That year, the peace accords were signed ending the armed military conflicts that had originally brought so many Salvadorans to the United States a decade earlier. The end of the war in El Salvador was something we had all been waiting for. We paid a high price. Over 75,000 people died, including my three brothers, and thousands were disappeared. Me and my colleagues worked especially hard to ensure that CARECEN could play a leading role in helping the U.S.-based Salvadoran community through the changes that affected them and their families back home at this historic moment. We started important initiatives to accomplish these aims and did a lot of significant work in this area. As the person mainly responsible for communicating our efforts to Salvadoran community members, I was at work non-stop during this period.

Unexpected local events would soon only increase my workload. In late April 1992, Los Angeles experienced the worst urban riot in modern American history following the initial court ruling in the Rodney King police beating case that gained worldwide attention. Mayor Tom Bradley, the city's longtime but soon-to-be-retired mayor, decided to respond by assembling a high-level citizen's committee to develop a rebuilding program for Los Angeles. Somewhat to my surprise, I was named to the committee, which was known as Rebuild L.A.

Rebuild L.A., headed by former U.S. Olympics Commissioner Peter Ueberroth, was a large committee of mostly very powerful southern Californians. These were primarily politically connected business and civic leaders who constituted a Who's Who of Los Angeles. My unlikely involvement in the organization's work helped to expand my vision and appreciation of what we, the Central American people, were capable of achieving in U.S. society. We started to speak of the necessity to get involved in economic development initiatives to benefit our community, such as community investment and low-income housing strategies, the establishment of financial institutions, the creation of small businesses and family loan funds, etc. And we began working to make these things happen.

In order to advance this agenda, I enrolled in a training program at UCLA to prepare myself to become a community economic development expert. In conjunction with the program, I traveled to Germany to learn about models and initiatives there that we might replicate in our communities in Los Angeles. Upon my return from Germany, we commenced the process to buy a building for CARECEN with the help of then Los Angeles Councilman Mike Hernández. Thanks to the support of Rebuild L.A., moreover, we were also able to secure private funds for CARECEN and other nonprofit agencies to bring new hope and opportunities to the neglected communities affected by the riots.

All of this work helped to strengthen CARECEN's public standing and influence. I am very proud of what we were able to accomplish as a result of that. Today, CARECEN remains one of the Latino community's strongest and most influential institutions in southern California and in the nation. The five years that I spent working there helped to deepen my awareness of the possibility and the importance of building strong U.S.-based institutions to promote Salvadoran community advancement. When the war ended in El Salvador, many of us logically started to ask ourselves, “Should we stay in the United States, or return to El Salvador?” Many of us continued to think that we wanted to leave, but in reality our work in this country was still very much needed and we had already invested many years of hard work here to establish ourselves as a community. As a result, most of us decided to stay in the United States.

Having decided to remain in California, I began to consider other things that I might be able to do to help the Salvadoran community integrate into the mainstream of U.S. civic and public life. I focused especially on the need for more strategic investment in our community’s leadership development, education and political participation and representation. In the years during which we had been settling in this nation as a refugee population, many of our initial wave of newcomers had established families here.

Since 1980, we had gone through a transition from an unknown, unsophisticated refugee community, to a more legally and economically established and integrated community comprised of first- and second-generation Salvadorans, many of whom had U.S.-born children and many of whom had become naturalized U.S. citizens with the right to vote. But our people, and especially our younger people, despite the benefits of citizenship, were nevertheless growing up in relative spiritual and material impoverishment. They knew little about their families’ histories in El Salvador. In addition, they were developing in many cases only very limited English language skills and most of our young people were attending schools that typically failed to address their needs. All of this concerned me and other first-generation leaders as we thought about the implications for building a next generation of leadership.

In 1995, in order to respond to these challenges, I founded a new organization. With the support of various friends who joined me in this new endeavor, we established La Organización Salvadoreña Americana (the Salvadoran American Organization), or OSA. Later, in 1998, we changed our name to the Salvadoran American Leadership and Educational Fund, or SALEF. Our aim was to target Salvadoran Americans and especially those who no longer needed immigration services, English classes or social services. We were especially interested in appealing to the next generation of community members who, building on the good work of existing anchor organizations, could help to extend our reach to important new domestic issues, such as education, public policy, voting and political participation and representation.

Since SALEF's inception, we have organized our work around two main issues: education and political empowerment. Consistent with these concerns, we have provided over 400 scholarships to underserved Salvadoran and other Latino students, providing assistance and incentives to our youth and future generations to access educational opportunities in greater numbers. We have also supported and advocated for political representation of Salvadorans in leadership positions on commissions and boards at the local and state levels. Despite our many gains over the years, political empowerment continues to be a key imperative for our community. SALEF has responded by advancing important voter education and non-partisan registration campaigns.

Thanks to this work, we have seen great increases in Salvadoran community engagement in recent local, state and national campaigns. We have seen real improvement in the number of Salvadorans going to the polls on Election Day, and in the sophistication of Salvadoran voters once they get to the voting booth. Nationwide today, there is more awareness than ever within our community about the nature and importance of participating in the U.S. political process. There is also greater mutual respect between city and state leaders and the Salvadoran community.

I am especially satisfied that SALEF has played such a significant role in involving more Salvadorans in the U.S. voting process. This work has greatly enhanced our ability to shape policy in the places where we are most concentrated in this country, and especially in Los Angeles which has the largest concentration of Salvadoran Americans than any other U.S. city. As a result of the successes of our organization, Los Angeles's new mayor, Antonio Villaraigosa, recently named me to serve on his transition team. I believe this is a concrete result of all the work that Salvadoran community members have undertaken over the years to establish ourselves as a contributing and important ethnic group in this country.

Building on all of these accomplishments, SALEF's current priorities include securing increased Salvadoran representation on city and state commissions, encouraging more Salvadoran community leaders to position themselves for key elected and appointed offices, and generating increased public appreciation of the Salvadoran American community's many contributions to North American economy and culture. I am optimistic about where we are going in the future as a community. Consequently, I want to continue working on building our social, political and economic power so that politicians of all stripes learn to gain even greater respect for us.

I would also like to see more Salvadorans in leadership positions. I would like to encourage even more of our people to become active in politics. I would also like to see more Salvadorans graduating from the best universities in this country. Whatever the arena—and different people will naturally choose different paths—what is most important is that our people advance. We need to create new opportunities for Salvadorans to own their homes, to receive more quality education, to have access to better paying jobs and to become more full participants in U.S. civic life. As an organization, I would like for SALEF to continue playing a leading role in these areas. Most concretely, I would like for us to establish an endowment so that we can further expand our scholarship support and our community impacts. That is my dream.

On a personal level, I suppose I will not feel completely satisfied until I complete my college studies. Perhaps one of the most difficult realities facing people like me who have forever been in the struggle is the many uncompensated personal sacrifices we have had to make along the way. I have never stopped working for peace and justice since the day I arrived in the United States, now nearly thirty years ago. I dream one day of taking a couple of years off on a sabbatical to finish my college studies and to spend time with my mother and family. At times I feel incomplete for not having been able to achieve more academically. On the other hand, I realize there is more to life than that. For example, I recently started a family, so these days I feel more complete as a human being than ever before. I now have my beautiful wife, Ana Elizabeth, and my beautiful son, Diego Valentino; they bring a healthy perspective and a sense of priority to everything I do these days.

When I reflect back on all that I have shared here, I am most drawn to the sacrifices of my mother in El Salvador and the many hardships she endured to enable my survival and success over the years. She grew up in poverty and disadvantage. She endured years of my father's alcoholism and then lost him at an early age to his addiction. She raised her eleven children essentially on her own. She lost a child when she was young. She lost three more of her children to the war in our country. And, then, even after the war's conclusion, she lost two more of her children in a single year, just four months apart. My mother is a strong woman and an emblem of our people's enduring spirit and will. When people ask me who my hero is, I say without hesitation that she is. God bless her.

Glossary of Organizations

Asociación de Estudiantes Latinoamericanos / Latin American Student Association is a San Francisco solidarity organization founded in the late 1970s to support the people of El Salvador, specifically students.

Asociación General de Estudiantes Universitarios Salvadoreños (AGEUS) / University Salvadoran Student Association. Founded in the 1960s in El Salvador, this organization was formed by university students as a response to the political situation in El Salvador. They did demonstrations as well as lobby work at different levels.

Asociación Nacional de Educadores Salvadoreños "Andes 21 de Junio" / National Association of Salvadoran Educators "Andes 21 de Junio" was formed at the end of the 1960s to protect the rights and improve the benefits of teachers at a national level in El Salvador.

Ayuda Médica para El Salvador / Medical Aid for El Salvador is a North American solidarity organization created in 1984 that facilitated medical supplies, medicine, preventive treatment and care to El Salvador. It also sent delegations.

Casa Farabundo Martí / Farabundo Martí House is a Salvadoran solidarity organization formed in San Francisco in 1981.

Center for Central American Studies Program at Cal State University, Northridge. The Central American Student Association (CAUSA), professors from the Chicano Studies and Humanities departments and members of the Central American community joined in a collective effort to create the first degree-granting program on Central American Studies in Los Angeles in the fall of 1999.

Centro Latino Cuscatlán / Cuscatlán Latin Center is a San Francisco organization that started in 2004 as a coalition to increase community representation in support of a legal status in the United States.

Centro de Recursos Centroamericanos / Central American Resource Center (CARECEN) is a legal and social services organization that advocates for the immigrant rights of the Central American Community in Los Angeles. It was founded in 1983.

Clínica Monseñor Oscar A. Romero / Monseignor Oscar A. Romero Clinic provides medical and dental services to the Central American community at large. It was founded by the Santana Chirino Amaya Refugee Committee and the Southern California Ecumenical Council of Churches in Los Angeles on August 11, 1983.

Comité Centro Americano de Trabajadores y Estudiantes / Central American Worker and Student Committee is a solidarity committee with the people of El Salvador that was formed in San Francisco during the 1970s to support students and workers by sending delegations and inviting representatives from their organizations to speak in the United States.

Comité Ernesto Jovel / Ernesto Jovel Committee was formed in Los Angeles in 1981 to update the Salvadoran community on events in El Salvador. It fundraised through music, tamale sales and parties to support union workers in El Salvador.

Comité Farabundo Martí / Farabundo Martí Committee is a solidarity committee with El Salvador that was formed in San Francisco and Los Angeles in 1981 to promote information about events in El Salvador; it also promoted culture through music and other events.

Comité de Refugiados Centroamericanos / Central American Refugee Committee (CRECE) was founded in Los Angeles and San Francisco in 1983. It started as a place for the community to gather and obtain immediate help as they arrived to the United States.

Comité de Refugiados Centro Americanos Santana Chirino Amaya / Santana Chirino Amaya Refugee Committee (SCARC) evolved from the Ernesto Jovel Committee in Los Angeles in 1983 and it started as a response to the overwhelming number of Salvadorans emigrating. It offered clothes, food, legal and medical references.

Cooperativa de Ahorros y Crédito Comunidades / Communities Credit and Savings Cooperative is an economic development project of El Rescate and it was founded in 1997. It started as a response to the economic needs of the community to assist with basic checking and saving accounts and small loans for students and entrepreneurs.

Fondo de Educación y Liderazgo Salvadoreño / Salvadoran American Leadership Educational Fund (SALEF) was created in 1995 to promote educational advancement in civic participation, leadership and economic prosperity of Salvadorans and other Latino communities in the United States.

Frente Democrático Revolucionario / Revolutionary Democratic Front (FDR) is a coalition of popular organizations and political parties in El Salvador that was formed in 1980. It started as a response to the political situation in El Salvador.

Frente Farabundo Martí para la Liberación Nacional / Farabundo Martí National Liberation Front (FMLN) is a coalition of four popular revolucionary forces in El Salvador that organized on October 10, 1980. It started as an alternative of political strength to oppose the oppression from the Salvadoran government.

Fundación de Ayuda Humanitaria e Investigación y Educación para El Salvador / Salvadoran Humanitarian Aid, Research and Education (SHARE) provided material and accompaniment to the Salvadoran refugees coming back from Honduras in 1987.

Instituto para el Desarrollo de la Nueva Democracia El Salvador-Estados Unidos / Institute for the Development of New Democracy USA-El Salvador is a binational project formed in San Francisco in the 1990s. It started as a way to explore the ways in which democracy can work after a civil war.

Médicos Solidarios / Solidarity Doctors is a solidarity group from San Francisco that provided medical supplies and services to different communities in El Salvador. It was founded in 1989.

Nuevo El Salvador Ahora / New El Salvador Today (NEST) is a Sister City and accompaniment solidarity project that was founded in San Francisco in 1987.

El Pulgarcito Rojo / The Little Red Thumb was a community newspaper that circulated in San Francisco in the 1980s.

El Rescate / The Rescue is a community-based organization that provided legal and social services and advocated for the immigrant's rights of Salvadorans in Los Angeles. It was founded in 1981.

Universidad Nacional de El Salvador (UES) / National University of El Salvador is the first academic institution in El Salvador founded on February 16, 1841.